FATHERS OF EUROPE

PATRIOTS OF PEACE

By The Same Author :—

UNFINISHED HISTORY

FATHERS OF EUROPE

PATRIOTS OF PEACE

Robert Wendelin Keyserlingk

PALM PUBLISHERS LIMITED
MONTREAL

First published by Palm Publishers Ltd.
Montreal, Canada in 1972

ISBN 0-919366-18X

Produced in Great Britain

Introduction

It has been said that history, like journalism, is a record not merely of what has happened but of what has mattered. All recorded happenings must, because of their very abundance, undergo a process of selection for the purposes of narrative. There can, however, be no selection without evaluation. Since all evaluation presupposes criteria, values and therefore judgment, there must also be a wide range of opinion on what really matters.

Once one admits that all historical records, all historical writing and all day-to-day reporting must be selective, the consequences of this selective process must also be clearly set forth. The selective process is dominated by two most powerful forms of opinion shaping. One is today's recording of events as represented by modern journalism. The other is the record of past events, namely, history. Neither can be considered as objective since both are selective and therefore subjective. Once selection becomes necessary, subjectivity alone decides what has mattered. We naturally take for granted the accuracy of today's or yesterday's record. We only deal with the evaluation of facts, not with the embroidery of fiction. But too often mere accuracy of reporting is no guarantee of the accurate presentation of an event. There always remains the element of subjective selectivity, depending upon what has mattered most, and to whom.

Some humourist once said that the pessimist is the historian who projects his hopes into an idealised past and projects his frustrations into the future. The optimist, the same humourist claims, condemns the past and creates his dream world in the future. If, therefore, to some extent all contemplation of the past as well as of the future is not unrelated to a person's predilection, with subjective judgments and temperamental proclivities playing their part, there is still a very important third approach. This third approach is to seek from the past sufficient experience in the hope of gaining some wisdom for the present and future. It is this search we are now engaged in.

A person or a society without a sense for or a knowledge of history has rightly been compared to a person suffering from amnesia. It must be remembered that the danger of amnesia is to be found not merely in lack of memory, but also in a consequent loss of factual knowledge, wisdom and hence judgment. Neither judgment nor wisdom can really be exercised without memory of previous experience, merely by intuition. The sufferer from amnesia can carry on very satisfactorily all his physical and mental functions when facing an immediate situation; his reactions to heat, cold and even to certain forms of danger become reflexive. But as soon as experience becomes necessary for an adult, mature and reasonable judgment leading to a wise decision, the loss of memory can be fatal.

In an age where "image-forming" by the most powerful technical means of fact-finding, namely the ability to transmit facts by sound, picture and printed word in all the various forms of display, from large type to piercing noises or garish colours, to enhance or minimise importance, the modern individual is constantly forced to make an evaluation of what really matters.

Having spent a life-time watching and, as a journalist, recording history in the making involving three generations, it is increasingly clear to me that we have quite a gap today between credulity and credibility. What might not be a true picture might still be an accurate enumeration of some facts. Such a picture need contain no inaccuracy since its sin is not one of commission, but merely of omission of very vital additional facts or explanations. Modern propaganda has long abandoned the cruder efforts of a Northcliffe, who had Germans manufacturing soap from cadavers, or Communists convincing the gullible of cannibalism as practised by the bourgeoisie. There are quite enough facts available, thanks to modern communications, to pick and choose from and to make an entirely false presentation. This was the modern achievement of Nazi propaganda.

The worship of "fact" and "documentary evidence" needs considerable debunking in the public mind. Working on the old adage that seeing is believing, modern man is now faced with the necessity of developing his critical faculties to the point of realising that he can practically see too much to understand all he sees, and that the brevity of his life will prevent him from seeing all that there is to be seen. Just as figures cannot lie but liars can figure, man can today manipulate figures, documents, including pictures, to serve varying specific ends. There are today enough facts of past events available to furnish any kind of "proof" required for almost anything.

The value of facts even in court proceedings varies according to the judgment of a society or a regime. The absurdity of a mixed court of Western and Soviet judges, became obvious immediately after World War II. Maybe a story, even if apocryphal, told about the Soviet member of the panel of judges during the Nuremberg trials illustrates this point. The Soviet knew that precious archives and records could be exploited to falsify a given picture. They had had long practice in that. In their judgment there was no convincing legal point involved in the question of political crimes, for they had committed most of these themselves. Therefore General Rudenko, the Soviet judge, when asked by a Western colleague, heavily burdened with bulging files, why he had come into court carrying no brief of details against the accused, answered: "Me? Brief? I have no brief, only a list!" and he drew from his pocket a single sheet of paper with the names of all the accused. Rudenko needed no elaborate file as a prelude to pre-determined executions. For him only one fact established legality: being the stronger.

In his Introduction to a prodigious history of England, of which only the first volume was published before the author's death, Douglas Jerrold argues that the most illuminating books on history were those written by men who had lived through the times they described, especially when they had been actively involved in them as diplomats, statesmen and writers. He reasons that unless one could also tell which of the events at a certain time influenced developments in a certain direction, one could not accurately evaluate the importance of those incidents of history. Any later researcher could obviously collate all the facts, but in his narrative of a trend, a development, a historical sequence like war, revolution or power changes, it is too easy to miss the main factors. They influenced overpoweringly at the time, but out of context, to a subsequent generation, these same facts might appear as trivial or quite unimportant. How often have we in the Free World heard people equating the existence of a totalitarian regime with popular approval. To a good but historically ignorant democrat nobody would stand such political oppression unwillingly. It is very difficult for a person living in freedom and security to imagine what a machine-gun in the hands of a small but ruthless police force in a totalitarian state really means. But by the same token it is equally difficult in a mass age of technology to realise that the personal human element can still be stronger than physical factors. Evaluating political facts against an exacting scale of historical knowledge also means accepting conviction and strong principles as historical realities.

It is against this background, conscious of the masses of written records, that I have undertaken to add another. As foreign correspondents we had to sift through tens of thousands of words daily, recording hundreds of events of varying significance in the country to which we were accredited. From all we read, heard and saw we had to select, according to the criteria of our judgment, that which mattered sufficiently to warrant expensive cables being sent for world-wide distribution. Here I have used the same technique for selecting out of records of many years that which to my mind has mattered enough not only for yesterday's headline, but for the coming generations who will have to live with that history which I saw in the making. It is for them to cope with, whether they use it or ignore it. But one thing is certain—they can only ignore it at their peril. The effects will be much more exacting in their generation. My generation has already suffered so greatly by its neglect of the truth about man. It could have learned better than it did. But it has already paid the price in suffering. History will show whether it was a fee paid in full for the lessons learned or merely a down-payment for a lesson taught but not accepted by the truant.

Contents

CHAPTER I

The Perils of Victory

THE Free World, led by the British Empire in its resistance and by the United States in its victory, had crushed Nazi and Fascist totalitarianism in Central and Southern Europe in 1945. But the Free World permitted considerable amputation of once free territories by Red totalitarianism and abandoned millions of once free people in Europe and Asia to continued political tyranny.

Contrary to Talleyrand's dictum that nations should do one another most good in peace and least possible harm in war, unconditional surrender had left the better part of the Western half of Europe in ruins, with the bulk of the Western European population, freed from Nazism, a political vacuum. The Eastern half, which had been occupied by Soviet troops, was also in ruins, but there Joseph Stalin took control. As water seeks to reach its own level, so political forces adjoining a political vacuum exhibit the same tendency. Every indication existed that Germany, Italy and even France would be taken over by their domestic Communist parties, powerfully backed by Soviet Russia. While Franklin Roosevelt still looked to Joseph Stalin as a new-found friend with whom he would build a new order, Stalin had his own political order in mind for the entire world.

The United States diplomat George Kennan, Head of the Planning Staff of the United States' State Department, commented in his memoirs, after having participated at the Moscow meeting between Secretary of State James Byrnes, British Foreign Secretary Ernest Bevin and Soviet Foreign Affairs Commissar Vyacheslav Molotov, that he had nothing but contempt for efforts to bring a semblance of freedom to a liberated Europe by trying to "preserve figleaves of democratic procedures to hide the nakedness of Stalin's dictatorship". Kennan was appalled by the Allies' lack of determined plans to counteract the definite programmes and antagonisms incorporating "the full vigour of Stalinist totalitarianism".

But the United States and the rest of the world, mortally endangered by greedy, victorious Communism emerging as the sole clear-cut alternative for millions in Europe, Asia and Africa, and even attracting the masses in the Caribbean and the Americas south of the Rio Grande, were to be spared the struggle of a third world war which might then have had a dubious outcome.

Three men came to the fore. They emerged from comparative obscurity to overcome strong initial opposition, even from the Allied military rulers of their recently liberated countries. They assumed civilian government responsibilities, fortified only by the fervent faith with which they challenged Communist ideology, namely, their Christian convictions.

Konrad Adenauer created a political party out of political ruins in Germany. After a long career of public service in his home town, Cologne, he made his post-war national political début after being ousted and banned from civic office by the British Military Government.

Alcide De Gasperi overcame the suspicions of the military government in Italy, where the Western Allies and the Soviet policy cooperated in rehabilitating Italian Communists. He was suspect both to the Italian Marxists as well as to the Italian Liberals because of his Christian convictions, and hence seemed a dubious political ally to the representatives of the Western democracy.

Robert Schuman, French patriot and devout Christian, active for many years in the Catholic movement of his native Lorraine, emerged in France after narrowly escaping de Gaulle's purge. In successive French governments he became Finance Minister, Foreign Minister and later Premier. He gave an impetus and direction to politics which again made possible the hope of a free and united Europe. Finally ousted by his own countrymen, mainly by de Gaulle, he laid foundations in the Schuman Plan for future generations of Europeans.

The three men did not know each other at the beginning of their careers. There is a letter available in which Schuman expresses regrets to Alcide De Gasperi that they had met so late in life, after World War II. The Nazis tried to prove when they arrested Schuman that he had been conniving with Konrad Adenauer, because they both belonged to Catholic parties in their homeland. Actually, Schuman and Adenauer also met after the war for the first time when Schuman had become Foreign Minister of the Fourth Republic of France.

But they had all three been formed in their youth by the Catholic social movements activated by the papal teachings of *Rerum Novarum*. They were all deeply religious, fervent patriots but determined antinationalists. All three came from frontier areas of border disputes and border contacts. Adenauer came from the Rhineland. De Gasperi was a native of the Trentino and Schuman, born in Luxemburg, in exile from his native Lorraine after German occupation in 1870, was a citizen of Metz. This had taught them that only Europe as a federation, not Europe torn by the hatreds bred by narrow nationalism, could assure freedom and liberty to their beloved, more intimate border homelands. They were political frontiersmen.

In his work as journalist and foreign correspondent, the author came to know all three, to follow their work, to question them and ponder their answers. Each one has been dealt with biographically or auto-biographically, but in their history and in their policies there is a deeper meaning than mere sequence; their very lives contain lasting implications for present struggles. That is the *leitmotiv* of this book.

Throughout the Free World we see today a revival of the old national and social antagonisms. Often unwittingly, such antagonisms engender the intellectual and political progeny: the almighty totalitarian state. These antagonisms are again bidding for position, under new names perhaps, but unmistakable. How much of what is now proclaimed as technological break-through in social engineering and has been given unchallenged sway as technocratic efficiency, was rightly seen by these men as the dehumanising state planning of totalitarian purpose. Yesterday the aim was to raise the individual as a mere functional unit so that he could be "rightly directed" by an all-knowing state. Today's state planners seem equally sure of the correct rules to which individuals should conform, from procreation to production.

The lesson taught by Adenauer, De Gasperi and Schuman as exponents and practitioners of fundamental concepts of a Christian society, is but a memory to some, and ignored by thousands to whom the struggle of thirty years ago is a by-gone incident and therefore irrelevant history. In actual fact, it becomes more apparent every day that the issue these three men confronted again confronts the rising generation. Political reality today is somewhat obscured by "groovy" slogans designed to present the hitherto shocking as desirable. The three men saw the insidious threat to personal liberty in their day, because they were trained to recognise the age-old challenge to man's freedom by ever-aspiring tyrants. They knew the challenger: man's inordinate desire for power when uncurbed by firm acceptance of clear moral restraints.

Emerging independently from internal political collapse in the three principal Western nations of Europe, these men are probably the most interesting political phenomena of the twentieth century. There have been more colourful and potent individuals. Maybe the men who emerged from the collapse of Russia after World War I and effected the transformation of theoretical Western Marxism into the applied Marxism of the Bolshevik dictatorship of Russia, can dispute their rank in the impact of the political developments they generated. Winston Churchill and Franklin Roosevelt have also marked their epoch. But in constructively pointing the way towards peaceful means of growth, the subjects of this book have a unique position.

Schuman saw France collapse in 1940. France's Third Republic first crumbled politically. Then the military impact of Germany crushed her military as well as governmental structure. For years the influence of the French communist party, led by Maurice Thorez, had been a major factor and led eventually to the left wing majority coalition of the Front Populaire under Léon Blum, the Socialist leader. But it must be remembered that while Léon Blum, both as a socialist and as a Jew, was a determined and courageous opponent of Nazi ambitions, his Marxist colleague Maurice Thorez took his orders from Moscow. Frequent assignments to Paris in those days presented me rare opportunities to notice how the political scandals, vying with financial ones, were sapping the fibre of the "bourgeois" parties. A largely venal press was verging on the blatant in advocacies of policies formulated outside France. One was watching a dismal decay of political, social and moral ethics, without which a parliamentary democracy cannot survive.

One of the more immediate causes for final French collapse was the not unexpected result of the newly found friendship between Stalin and Hitler, as formulated in the Ribbentrop-Molotov non-aggression pact. Joseph Stalin agreed to partition Poland with Hitler and directed the communist parties—particularly that of France—to abandon their bitter enmity to National Socialist aggression. When Hitler's armies attacked France, Maurice Thorez, the communist leader, proclaimed the rightness of Hitler's cause in resisting the "imperialist war-mongers of Washington and London" and appealed to French workers and soldiers not to fight. He had to flee to Moscow to avoid a traitor's death but the damage done to French morale in sapping the will to resist was immense.

Historians will argue for many years whether Marshal Pétain, inheriting the sorry mess from the pre-war politicians, was right when he accepted military defeat after the French army collapsed, and whether he saved France for ultimate survival and assured Hitler's defeat by establishing a Vichy government. Pétain succeeded in deflecting Hitler's armies from a total occupation of France. He placed obstacles in Hitler's path to an unhampered assault on Africa and even on Britain. A full-scale French puppet government, which was a possibility in the mood which prevailed in France at the time, could have brought aid to Hitler. Instead the Nazis faced a constant slow sabotage, not only from the maquis, but also from Marshal Pétain, whose prestige was great enough to prevent Hitler riding roughshod over his Government, which could hardly have resisted the uninhibited force of Nazi arms.

It is important to remember these facts when appraising the role of Robert Schuman in the France of 1945. He, like De Gasperi and Adenauer, had to fill a political vacuum with a fervent, unswerving conviction which could be translated into a political force. This force proved sufficiently potent first to block and then to defeat the victorious march of Communism across Europe impelled by the strength of a surging Red Army able to rely on effective Fifth Columns of obedient communists.

Of all the Western Allies only Canada maintained an ambassador to the Pétain Government at Vichy, Pierre Dupuy. His visits to London and Ottawa during that period furnished invaluable information. On several of these occasions he told me how Marshal Pétain exercised a form of passive resistance against the Nazis, blocking and impeding their efforts to fully exploit their military victory over France, which if successful might have had fateful results for the Allies. We were not allowed to write about these aspects lest Dupuy's mission be frustrated, but it was Churchill himself who considered this direct contact with Vichy a valuable avenue for intelligence as well as direct military strategy. Publication of Dupuy's own memoirs, about which he told me several years before his death, has been constantly postponed, but will doubtlessly throw interesting light on the full rôle Pétain played, should they appear.

Germany collapsed as a political entity several years after France; and there Konrad Adenauer emerged with the task of establishing government in a political vacuum. But it was in Italy, which had been under a totalitarian dictatorship much longer than either Germany or Nazi occupied France, that the biggest political adjustment had to be made. Italy had an entire generation which had come of age educated by Mussolini. In a way she had been the birthplace of Fascism, the Western brand of political marxist Socialism.

Political scientists have sometimes attempted to see a unique quality in Bolshevism, because it preaches world revolution and the universal emancipation of the masses, while its kin, Fascism and Nazism, restrict themselves to schemes for nationalistic domination. Such attempts at differentiation overlook two important features, basic ideology and practical experience. To Bolshevism, Nazism and Fascism, man is but a functional unit in a materialist collective, whether it be called a Union of Socialist Republics or an Empire;

fulfilment is to be sought in collective salvation, through the establishment of the dictatorship of a group, a class or a nation. All these are arbitrary, semantic descriptions of a sociological figment of the imagination, namely, the collective as a decision maker. In actual fact, the collective, the mass, is but material to be moulded, directed or even led by an individual or a group of individuals, in their turn governed by individual wills. The mortal rivalry between Fascism, Nazism and Bolshevism was not really one of ideological differences, but a family feud, its members rivalling for the attainment of totalitarian world power.

Italy had been the first victim of a totalitarian dictatorship in Western Europe, and also produced after its collapse the most interesting and in many ways, the best intellectually prepared leader to come out of the political rubble in defeated and war-scarred Italy—Alcide De Gasperi.

Chapter II

The Emerging Issue—Its Background

De Gasperi was born on April 3rd, 1881, the son of Amadeo Degasperi[1] and Maria Morandini, at Pieve Tesino, where his father Amadeo was in command of the local border Police detachment of the Austrian Empire. Later his father was transferred to Civezzano, where young Degasperi received his first schooling from Canon Victor Merler, an enlightened man who had great influence on his pupils. It is important to remember that Alcide De Gasperi, one of Italy's great patriots, was born an Austrian citizen, at a time when his home province of Upper Adige and the Trentino region were part of the Austrian Empire. Actually the Trentino had never belonged to Italy since Italy, as a unit, was only established in 1861. But while ruled by Italian, German and other princes and by the French under Napoleon, it had for centuries had an Italian population. The Trentino came under Austrian rule after Napoleon was defeated, by the terms of the Treaty of the Congress of Vienna in 1815.

There was a specially difficult situation on this frontierland. Nationality, religion and cultural roots were all very closely intertwined.

There existed strange conflicts and even contradictions. Nationally the attraction of language and culture was toward the new Kingdom of Italy. Yet politically and religiously the economic liberalism, the impediments to catholic education in a secularised society, dominated by the anti-clerical traditions of a Cavour and Garibaldi, did not enhance the prospects for political union with Italy among the basically conservative Trentino Italians. Many of them actually worked more to vindicate their minority rights as Italians within a Hapsburg Empire than to support separation from it and union with the Kingdom of Italy under the King of Savoy, who quarrelled with the papacy, and liberalised marriage laws and other traditions.

[1] It was only later that the more usual form of De Gasperi came into use.

This was the situation when De Gasperi began to take an active interest in the political life of his native Trentino. Already in 1897 as a 17 year old student, we see him advocating greater local autonomy and Italian minority rights, rather than actual secession and incorporation into the Italian state, avowedly anti-clerical and almost too new to be regarded as stable or politically viable. However, an Austrian security record of September 15th, 1898 shows that the police of Trent had placed his name on the list of "suspected Irredentists" who might advocate secession from Austria. Thus, from the very beginning De Gasperi, as a Christian Democrat (Popolari)[1] was faced with a kind of political war on two fronts. He fought against centralising initiatives from Vienna, inimical to the cultural character of his homeland, but he also took issue with the anti-religious policies of the Liberals and Socialists of the Trentino. All these parties were made up of Italians by nationality, Austrian by citizenship.

To add to the confusion, the Socialists assumed a pro-Italian stance in attacking De Gasperi because of his loyalty to the Church, claiming that to be Catholic meant to be pro-Hapsburg and hence pro-Austrian, while at the same time they themselves took a very active, if subordinate role, as an integral part of the Austrian Socialist Party. It is a matter of historical interest that De Gasperi's loyalty to his people and to his Church exposed him throughout his political career to contradictory attacks on his loyalty. He was on the police list as an Italian "Irredentist", yet not only the Socialists of the Trentino, but even the Fascist regime in later years, when De Gasperi had become an Italian citizen, tried to cast doubts on his loyalty to his own people. They too equated loyalty to the Church with loyalty to the Hapsburgs and Austria. A slightly closer examination of history will show to what extent the Hapsburg dynasty and the Church had been and still were at odds with each other. This became particularly apparent in the treatment of the Church in the Trentino during World War I.

Early in his life, De Gasperi began to write articles for the local paper *La Voce Cattolica* in Trent. Two or three times a week he discussed the social doctrine of the Church, on which he laid more emphasis than on questions of nationality in his polemics with Liberals and Socialists. These were often articles answering those in the Socialist *Popolo* which were particularly violent in their attacks against the Church.

It was in 1909, prior to his election to the Austrian Reichsrat in 1911, that De Gasperi first crossed swords with his bitter foe of later

[1] This party was inspired by the Christian social teachings of Don Luigi Sturzo.

years, Benito Mussolini. Mussolini had been sent by the Socialist Party of Italy to activate the campaign against the Popolari, and for about a year he campaigned in the Trentino, launching bitter personal attacks against De Gasperi. Mussolini had become editor of the Trent Socialist paper *Popolo*, while De Gasperi fought back as editor of the former *Voce Cattolica* which he renamed *Il Trentino*. Mussolini, the international Marxist, attacked De Gasperi as the supporter of nationality and religion, and himself supported the Austrian Socialist Party, closely linked with the German Socialists, and preaching the ideal of an anti-national Second International.

Some twenty-five years later, in 1934 I interviewed Benito Mussolini, then dictator of Italy, ensconced in his famous room in the Palazzo Venezia. By then he had become the most violent exponent of the narrowest form of nationalism, and was responsible for the murder of his former Socialist Party colleague, Matteotti. He had also had Alcide De Gasperi jailed, persecuted and declared an enemy of his Italian Fascist state.

Another twelve years later in 1946, I talked to Alcide De Gasperi, at the Palazzo Chigi. He was now responsible for leading Italy out of the misery into which she had been plunged by Mussolini: the latter had paid with his life for the chaos and violence he had spread amongst his people while he was il Duce. He thus personified the evolution of Socialism to dictatorship, witnessed by then in many other countries.

In the elections which brought De Gasperi to Vienna as a member of Parliament (*Reichsrat*) in 1911 he headed the Popolari (Christian Democrat) list, obtaining about 75 per cent of the votes in his riding of Fiemme, Primiero and Civezzano. The province of Trent elected a total of seven Popolari, one Socialist and one Liberal.

Long before attaining the age of thirty, which permitted him legally to present his candidature, De Gasperi was actively engaged in the battle for the Christian social doctrine, for the rights of his people, and for greater local autonomy within a federated empire. The interest he was to take in federation of various nationalities was already apparent. Such a federation was also strongly advocated by the large Slav minorities in the Austrian Empire, comprising Serbs, Croats, Slovenes, Czechs, Poles, Moravians and Rumanians, and by the Mohammedans of Bosnia and Herzegovinia. If one takes into account the autonomous Hungarian Kingdom within the Hapsburg-Austrian Empire and the non-German citizens, the German speaking rulers of Austria consisted only of a minority of the whole Austro-Hungarian Empire which was composed of some two dozen nationalities. Here was a good school for a man who was to play such an important role in striving for a united Europe.

During his student days in Vienna, De Gasperi participated in the establishment of an Italian-speaking students' union in Vienna, Innsbruck and Graz. He was actually arrested and detained in prison long enough to lose a whole semester of studies, when he participated in a student rally advocating an Italian university for Trent.

It was a bitter experience for this young patriot to find that while he was fighting the battle for local autonomy of the three Italian provinces within Austria,[1] great disunity was stirred up amongst his people by the various Italian groups on social and religious issues.

The Liberals attacked the Popolari for being too socialist, while the Socialists vehemently denounced the Christian programme of the Popolari as merely an anti-socialist manoeuvre of the Church to attract the masses away from Marxism.

In the Vienna Reichsrat, De Gasperi's activities in his formative years as a political leader were primarily directed towards the defence of his people and other non-German minorities within the Austro-Hungarian Empire. He co-operated with the sixty-three deputies of the German-speaking Christian Social Party of Austria on questions where Catholic teachings were involved or where Catholics were being attacked by the Socialists and the Liberals, particularly in matters of education and family legislation. The highest legislative body of Austro-Hungarian government was the so-called Delegation—a combined Second-Chamber consisting of delegates of the Austrian and Hungarian Parliaments. Basically, the Austro-Hungarian Empire was an authoritarian monarchy with many constitutional features, although of course its Parliament in no way compared with that within the constitutional monarchy of Great Britain, or the Scandinavian and some other West European monarchies.

De Gasperi was elected to the Delegation by the representatives of the Italian group in the Austrian Parliament in 1912. It was his membership in that body, as well as his parliamentary immunity as deputy, which permitted him to continue his political activities through the difficult years of 1914–18, when Austria and Italy were at war and the Italian and other minorities in Austria were subjected not only to suspicion but to considerable repression.

De Gasperi found himself in a particularly delicate position in the years just before World War I. As a member of the Austrian Parliament defending the rights of Italian nationals who were Austrian citizens, he was a point of embarrassment both to Rome and to Vienna. The new Italian state was joining Austria and Germany to

[1] Trentino, Friuli and Istria.

build the Triple Alliance. The Italian Government in Rome was obviously embarrassed and frequently had to disassociate itself from the Italian co-nationals under the Austrian crown who were defending their *Italianità* against the germanising efforts of the Vienna Government and who were encouraged by the not too discreet applause of German nationalists within the neighbouring Hohenzollern Reich of Germany. But De Gasperi's difficulties were increased when Italy later reneged on her support of the Central powers against the other Triple Alliance, France, Great Britain and Russia. Rome's attitude aroused the ire of the government in Vienna, not only against Italy, but also against the citizens of Italian language and culture within the Austrian Empire.

As tension rose between the rival triple alliances, with Germany, Austria and Italy on the one side and France, Great Britain and Russia on the other, Italy veered away from her Austro-German allies. In this situation it was De Gasperi's desperate hope that peace would prevail, lest his Italian people in Austria should find themselves in the middle of a conflict not only destructive to their border homeland, but also pitting Austrian-Italians against Italians from the Kingdom of Italy.

He made special visits to Rome where he had lengthy meetings with the Italian Foreign Minister, Giorgio Sonnino and also conferred with Pope Benedict XV, who was at that time deeply involved in peace efforts with his offers of mediation between the opposing groupings. Here was another curious contradiction of political life. Sonnino was one of Italy's most violent anti-clericals and went to all sorts of lengths to thwart the Pope's peace initiatives. At the same time he welcomed efforts at mediation by De Gasperi as Catholic deputy from Vienna. But on April 26th, 1915 in London, when Sonnino finally signed the secret treaty with the Western allies, by which Italy ranged herself against the Central Powers, he insisted on the insertion of a secret clause. This was to the effect that under no circumstances would the victorious Allies permit the Holy See to be represented at any consequent peace conferences. The Italian Government later tried to justify this by arguing that the internal cohesion of Italy demanded an anti-clerical and particularly anti-papal attitude. All this goes to show how difficult De Gasperi's position was, as he tried to navigate between the various policies. When Italy did not join in the declaration of war against the Western Allies, he urged Vienna and Berlin to accept a non-belligerent Italy as a neutral. He was hoping that Rome's diplomacy would induce Vienna to desist from its policy of oppression and germanisation practised against the Italians of the Trentino before the war, and accentuated when war actually did break out.

When Italy finally took up arms at the side of the Allies against Austria and Germany, the draconian measures against the Austrian citizens of Italian nationality became ferocious. On that day De Gasperi closed his Italian language paper *Il Trentino*, rather than publish anti-Italian communiqués. The last issue had a two-column headline, "Decision of the Italian Parliament" and below a blank space with just one word, "Censorship".

Thus at the outbreak of the war in 1914, Alcide De Gasperi, who had started his political activities as a student, now had fifteen years of practical experience behind him. Of himself, Adenauer, and Schuman, he had been most directly involved in international policies and was the one who had had to face the peculiar difficulties presented by the chequered pattern of nationalities within the Austrian Empire. One can readily see how a man of his intellectual background and social training would be preoccupied with the possibility of seeking understanding and peace between nationalities. He would know only too well that nationality, unlike political adherence to (often) juridical entities such as the modern state, is a real and lasting factor and one that cannot be abolished by decree.

The pre-World War I years saw Konrad Adenauer and Robert Schuman in far less exposed and internationally sensitive positions. Nevertheless, the problem of nationality, as a factor which had to be adjusted to larger and often foreign state structures, was also present.

Konrad Adenauer once described his career to his biographer, Paul Weymar in these words: "Come to think of it, I have lived not one, but three lives. The first leads up to the year 1917. The second comprises my period as Lord Mayor of Cologne. And the third—well, it began after the German collapse in 1945".[1]

Adenauer was born on January 5th, 1876 into the very modest surroundings of the family of Konrad Adenauer, clerk of the Cologne District Court and his equally devout Catholic wife Hélène Scharfenberg, daughter of a bank clerk in Cologne. The Chancellor's father, who started life as a farm labourer and brickworker after completing elementary schooling, enrolled as a soldier. He must have had special gifts, besides his sense of duty. After the battle of Koeniggraetz (Sadova), in which Prussia gained a victory over Austria on July 3rd, 1866 and in which he was wounded, he was granted a commission from the ranks for conspicuous bravery. This was an extremely rare event in the old Prussian army, and no easy matter. With his humble antecedents, to remain among the exclusive officers' caste was too difficult; hence his military career was short lived. He had decided to marry, a step for which an officer not only had to obtain permission,

[1] *Konrad Adenauer*, Paul Weymar (André Deutsch, London), page 13.

but had also to show sufficient financial resources, commensurate with the dignity of his new rank. Neither he nor his prospective father-in-law could indicate any such financial status. So Konrad Adenauer senior retired from the army as Lieutenant Adenauer and received a modest government position as court clerk. The position was so modest that the family income had to be supplemented, as the children began to arrive, by the mother's earnings as a seamstress, but the family managed to see three sons through university—no mean achievement at a time when many of today's government and private aids to students either did not exist, or were on a much more modest scale.

Before young Konrad began his law course, he had a short stint as a bank clerk, as university training for the two older ones had already strained the family exchequer considerably. But it became obvious that it was definitely not Konrad's vocation to remain a bank clerk, and a very special effort was made by the father to give his third son the same opportunity as the other two. With aid for tuition from a private foundation, established to help specially gifted boys, and a drastic cut in the family budget to pay for his board and lodging in Freiburg and later in Bonn, young Konrad was able to achieve his *referendar*, the first law degree, in the record time of three years. A year later Konrad passed his assistant judgeship qualifications (assessor) and received his first salary as a junior legal officer of the state. To augment his income he left government service and joined a legal firm, that of Dr. Kausen, who was not only the best civil lawyer at Cologne's High Court, but also leader of the Catholic Centre Party in the Cologne City Council. Adenauer's law practice was most successful, earning recognition and commensurate rewards. He now could make marriage plans with Emma Weyer, daughter of an old and well established family of the Cologne *haute bourgeoisie.* Emma's mother was a Wallraf. Max Wallraf was Lord Mayor of Cologne, and Konrad Adenauer eventually succeeded him, having served under him and received a very thorough training as a member of the City Council. By the time Max Wallraf was appointed Under Secretary of the Interior in Berlin in the summer of 1917, Konrad Adenauer was ready and stepped into the important position of Lord Mayor of Cologne.

Unless one follows the career of Konrad Adenauer on the City Council of his native city, there is as yet no political activity on a wider scale to record. But it must be remembered that the City of Cologne held a very special position within the Prussian state, had special rights of representation and fiscal privileges for trade and navigation, some of which dated back to the Middle Ages. Thus service on the City Council was more than ordinary city administration and gave a double experience. One was very close contact with government in general, the second the role Adenauer played as an active member in the Catholic Centre Party, which exerted considerable influence within the political spectrum of the metropolis of the Rhineland

The Catholic Centre Party, known as the *Zentrum,* was so thoroughly steeped in Catholic doctrine as to be the only party to encompass practically every stratum of society, from titled semi-feudal landowners to farm labourers, and from the industrial tycoon or professional to the labouring masses of the proletariat within the powerful Catholic trade unions. It directly challenged Karl Marx's classless society based on the dictatorship of the proletariat, by advocating a society in which classes were at peace with each other, united in a higher service, namely social justice as taught by the Church.

Through that teaching, we can trace the same influence on all three men, but first let us note the background of the third—Robert Schuman.

Robert Schuman was ten years junior to Konrad Adenauer and five years younger than De Gasperi. He was born in "exile". His father, Jean Pierre Schuman, was a medium land owner in the vicinity of Metz, in the Lorraine. He lived in the little township of Evrange on the Lorraine-Luxemburg border. In 1870 we find Schuman's father fighting in the French army against the Prussians, and he was captured when the French army collapsed at Sedan under the singularly inept leadership of Napoleon III. When the Prussians annexed Schuman's native Lorraine and it became a Prussian province,[1] the elder Schuman "exiled" himself to Luxemburg, purchasing a very comfortable but secluded rural residence in the village of Clausen, a suburb of Luxemburg City. Its very name indicated seclusion, as it was called the "Hermitage". From that villa, near the Malakov Tower, Jean Pierre Schuman managed his property on both sides of the border and there, on June 29th, 1886, an only child was born to him. Late in life he had married Eugenie Duren, twenty-five years his junior.

To emphasize the "borderland" tradition of the family, Robert Schuman's maternal grandfather Duren was a Customs official, a native of the same region as the Schumans. These people were as fervent in the maintenance of their local German dialect as they were in their French political and cultural allegiance. It is sometimes hard for Americans, belonging to the so-called New World, and for the British with their island tradition, to realise fully how

[1] The Schumans automatically becoming German citizens.

young most of the European political units actually are. The modern State is too often confused with a nationality. The history of these States frequently begins in the nineteenth century, or in the case of a few, in the eighteenth. The history of the British Monarchy and of the United States since they declared their independence in 1776, indicate a much longer continuity than the continent of Europe has generally seen.

This applies especially to the German people. In his series on the history of Italian people dealing with the period from the Caesars to the invasions by the various tribes of Goths, Indro Montanelli[1] speaks of the Franks, the Vandals and the Goths as "Germans". Political structures, monarchies and dukedoms came and went through the centuries in the many lands inhabited by German-speaking people, whether in Lorraine, Alsace, the Cantons of Switzerland, in the lands of the ancient Habsburg monarchies of Austria-Hungary down to Transylvania or the Baltic states like the Duchy of Courland, established early in the thirteenth century. It must be remembered that what is commonly known as the State of Germany was not established until 1871, only to be partly dismembered again in 1945. It never coincided with the actual geographic boundaries of German-speaking people, and certainly never comprised at any time all "the Germans".

This is an important factor in distiguishing political allegiance, namely citizenship, from nationality.

The struggle for national identity had been the story of De Gasperi's Trentino. It had been the story of Alsace-Lorraine, and of the Rhineland in the days of the Holy Roman Empire, when the Palatinate and the Low Countries, the electors and the dukedoms cherished and defended their autonomy. It was a continuous struggle for Adenauer's Cologne when it fell to Prussia in 1815, and from then on resisted the centralising bureaucracy of Prussian Berlin. Nationality meant to the vast majority of Europeans their limited "homeland", where the homogeneous society of language and often religion (from the old days when ruling princes applied the dictum *Cuius regio ejus religio*) gave life to a fervent patriotism but which was limited to that locality. However, this local patriotism did not preclude a genuine and even enthusiastic loyalty to the greater, often heterogeneous society of a modern state. Thus, for example, the German-speaking Courlander was a loyal subject of the Russian throne while resolutely resisting "russification" efforts by pan-slavistic enthusiasts in St. Petersburg. Since the older patriotisms based on nationality were usually centred on political or social

[1] *L'Italia dei Secoli Bui,* Montanelli, Roberto Gervase (Rizzoli, Milan, 1966), page 142.

entities whose direct roots drew strength and went back to paternalistic, feudal and definitely traditional soil, it was only natural that revolutionary egalitarian socialism saw in them an obstacle to political ambitions. Thus, the French Revolution and later the Bolshevik Revolution sought to establish centralised government as against federal government forms.

It should not, therefore, be a surprise that the third man to emerge in a post-war disrupted Europe rapidly drifting towards Communism, was also a product of precisely that milieu which Communists and Fascists tried for years to exterminate when they wished to remain masters of the situation.

Robert Schuman grew to school age in the secluded quiet of the Hermitage in the rural suburb of Clausen, where his mother, early widowed, devoted herself to his first lessons. Later at Luxemburg, he attended the classical college, the Atheneum. There Robert Schuman was able both to absorb his mother tongue of that particular German, also known as "Allemansch", which one finds with local variations all the way south to and including Switzerland, as well as to steep himself in the classical French which was the college's tradition.

His biographer Robert Rochefort[1] describes how young Schuman often recalled how it was that Luxemburg inspired his first stirrings of patriotism, when with his fellow students he could intone the defiant verses of the *Feirvon*, the national hymn of Luxemburg, whose lines "*Wir welle jo ken preisse sin*" (We do not want to be Prussians) were as fervently expressive for a Lorrainer as for a Luxemburger. And yet Rochefort emphasises that this flame of regional patriotism which had been awakened in a young exile never degenerated into the negative nationalism of a chauvinistic type which excluded appreciation of other lands and people.

On the completion of his secondary school studies the question arose as to the choice of a profession. At first Schuman seemed interested in pursuing an academic teaching career. But the consideration loomed large in his mind that to begin a teaching career, which would need to be in the Germany of the day (unless he wished to abandon his own people, which he did not) might conflict with his strong French attachments. So instead of teaching he decided to take up law and spent the following years at universities in Metz, Berlin, Bonn, Munich and Freiburg. He finally obtained his doctorate at the University of Strasbourg. It was a great help to him that he was exempted from military service on physical grounds and thus avoided another conflict of conscience.

[1] *Robert Schuman*, Rochefort (Cerf, Paris, 1968).

He often said in later years that it was his Alsatian friends at the University of Strasbourg who had made him really come to know France. He took a vivid interest in the political and hence national discussions there and also became a regular reader of the French language daily, *Le Nouveliste d'Alsace-Lorraine*, which, with singular tolerance from the Berlin Government, was published at Colmar and made no concessions in its columns when writing of "Our French Culture" using the term "their culture" when referring to Germany. He became a member of the Catholic Students' Association, UNITAS, which was also definitely oriented towards France. He was strongly influenced in later years by the close friendships formed there, particularly with Henry Eschbach and Paul Thiriet, both active in later years in the reintegration of Alsace-Lorraine into France.

But, recalling his student days during his first official visit as French Foreign Minister to Germany in 1950, he said to Konrad Adenauer in Bonn: "I think back on my personal experiences as a student in Bonn. Without realising what was awaiting all of us during this last half century, I laid the foundations for a considerable spiritual and intellectual enrichment, for I was able to ascertain by myself all that can be contributed to our common welfare by our co-operation".

Admitted to the practice of law in Metz and aided in this independence by his management of the family properties, Robert Schuman plunged into community work, taking an active part in church and social activities. These included the development of Catholic education under Prussian rule, and brought him into close contact with the vital elements of the French and German cultures which had been implanted in his native country.

In an article concerned with his own generation, written on the occasion of a commemorative study of Charles Frey, the former Mayor of Strasburg, Robert Schuman recalled how their principal knowledge of France was derived mainly from family traditions, which were sometimes the only source. Children received a biased picture of France, as presented by the German educational authorities who supplied the school manuals, and the large circulation dailies coming from the German centres pictured a very one-sided image of France to the Alsace-Lorraine population. It was, therefore, he recalls, the task of others like himself to play their role in maintaining the French tradition, "while obliged to adapt to the necessities of practical living and realistic attitudes, at the same time warding off any encroachment upon our principles and sentiments". Educational and Church activities were of equal concern to Schuman, as they deeply affected the very character of the people, who were as profoundly attached to their French cultural background as they were to their Catholic tradition, both of which received not infrequent challenges from a Prussian and Protestant administration. It must be remembered that when Alsace and Lorraine were incorporated into the newly founded German Reich by Bismarck they were directly attached as Prussian provinces under Berlin administration, while the former kingdoms Bavaria and Würtemberg, duchies such as Baden, and other principalities retained a certain amount of internal autonomy. This implied that Bismarck's attacks on the Catholic Church, the years of the so-called *Kulturkampf*, began as a very real aspect of Prussian policy in 1871. The *Kulturkampf* was pursued with vigour right up to 1877, continuing with varying degrees of intensity for more than a decade and was actually ended only when settlement was reached in 1891.

This struggle between Bismarck and the Catholic citizens of the newly formed Reich therefore was of equal importance to both the Rhineland and Alsace-Lorraine, to Adenauer and to Schuman. In tracing the career of these men it is hence of special interest to note their similar formative factors. It would be wrong to deduce from the intense interest that they shared with De Gasperi in the rôle of Catholic social teaching and Catholic doctrine, in their early youth, that they would have a restrictive militancy in matters of faith in later years. On the contrary, having experienced religious repression, they were particularly sensitive to religious intolerance without losing their fervour in the defence of principles for which they had stood from their earliest days.

Robert Rochefort deals with this point in his biography of Robert Schuman when he writes: "For Robert Schuman, as for Maurice Blondel, no earthly city, any more than any man, is an end in itself. The city, the nation, humanity are based on an obligation, reasonably and morally accepted by persons who can only develop by co-operation and devotion. It is the obligation of people who differ only among themselves as individual members of the same family differ from each other, rich in their diversities and in their agreements. Therefore no people has the right to eliminate or subjugate others, and the civil link between them all must be based upon confidence and friendship".[1]

In dealing with history it is idle to speculate what might have happened in different circumstances. But there is no doubt that when a political conquest is accompanied by religious differences, which are expressed in the efforts of the conquering or ruling elements to favour or even impose their own beliefs on the subjugated

[1] *Robert Schuman*, Rochefort (Cerf, Paris), page 80.

peoples, political resistance is immensely enhanced by an overtone of religious fervour. Not only was the Prussian administration of Alsace-Lorraine looked upon as a political "invader", it was also regarded as the active enemy of the religion of that land. Not only were there religious elements in Alsace-Lorraine's patriotic loyalty to France, the State from which it had been severed; patriotism in its turn deepened the spiritual influence of religion. This phenomenon of religious fervour coupled with secular loyalty to the homeland has been noted in other countries. Probably the clearest example is Poland, which had not only the Russian Orthodox government of the Tzars, but also the Russian Communist government to contend with, both combining political domination with religious interference.

There is no doubt that one of the strongest personal influences on Robert Schuman in the years preceding World War I was his mother. Left a widow early in life by a much older husband, with only the one son to bring up, this intellectually and spiritually gifted woman centred all her attention on him. In the correspondence between mother and son one finds frequent references to books she is suggesting he should read, and his comments on books he had read which would interest her. Theology and history were definitely the two subjects on which they were commenting most frequently. It was his mother who arranged for a pilgrimage to Lourdes so that her son could offer his thanksgiving for having again been exempted from military service by the military board. As Rochefort mentions in his biography of Schuman, Madame Schuman as a native of an annexed country, Lorraine, felt very deeply what this exemption meant. "If annexation had made a German citizen of Schuman, it had not made a German of him", and he, now, therefore, was saved from donning a German uniform.

Mother and son made a visit to Rome in 1909 to attend the beatification of Jeanne d'Arc, the patron saint of France. Schuman was on a walking tour in Switzerland with his friend Eschbach when his mother, thrown from a carriage when the coachman lost control of a run-away horse, was instantly killed on August 30th, 1911. It was a profound blow to Robert Schuman and contributed largely to his life during the next few years, when he devoted himself with special fervour to Church affairs and local political activities.

Schuman began to take an active part in the political group, known as the Volksverein, whose French name was *l'Union Populaire Catholique Lorraine*. The newspaper *La Croix de Lorraine* was edited by Canon Collin, a close friend of Schuman, who stood in the forefront of the religious and political battles. After a militant address at a meeting of the Volksverein on May 19th, 1913, Collin introduced for the first time the young lawyer Robert Schuman. "You already know 'Monsieur l'avocat Schuman'; that is a name honoured in politics because of his uncle, the member of the *Landtag* (provincial parliament) and respected even more because of his own activities at the Bar and in the social conflicts here. This introduction will suffice and I will pass you over to 'Monsieur l'avocat Schuman' ".

But it is only in 1918, upon the urging of his friends after the reincorporation of Alsace-Lorraine into the French state, that Schuman permits his name to go forward on an electoral list and is elected to the National Assembly in Paris.

Thus we see how De Gasperi, Adenauer and Schuman were deeply engaged even from their student days in political affairs, which had distinct and similar elements of patriotic and religious fervour, basically preoccupied as they were with the rights of the individual as against the State and those of the State as against the Church. We are faced even today with arguments over the demarcation line between what is God's and what is Caesar's. In the thirteenth century Innocent III claimed the right of the Church to challenge the authority of an Emperor, if he disregarded and disobeyed the laws of God. The same struggle continues in the twentieth century when secular rulers claim authority not only over men as citizens but over their conscience and religious allegiance.

Chapter III

The Issue Defined

Of the three men, De Gasperi made the largest contribution as scholar and writer to this particular conflict which is so characteristic of their political careers. To appreciate what they achieved against great odds, one must turn from day-to-day events to the thoughts and mainsprings of their actions. In an enlightening study of Catholic Social doctrine, especially *Rerum Novarum* and *Quadragesimo Anno*, De Gasperi deals with the evolution of corporatism and the political dangers involved in the mistaken use of good ideas.[1] He talks of the romantic period of corporatism, which later developed into syndicalism and the union movements of modern times. In 1865, Count Chambord, the Pretender to the French Throne, had published his *Lettre Publique aux Ouvriers*, in which the workers were urged to "unite in voluntary and regular free corporations to assure social harmony". The great social-reformist bishop of the nineteenth century, Baron Kettler, Archbishop of Mainz, was deeply conscious of the injustices towards the wage-earners practised by the economic liberalism of the entrepreneur, the early capitalist industrial society, and promoted the idea of corporate bodies to protect the workers against exploitation and society against a class war. It was in the matter of class war that the Catholic and Socialist social approach differed most profoundly, and the problem was not new.

The works of De Mun, la Tour du Pin, of Harmel, the French industrialist, establishing in his textile works of Val-du-Bois special profit-sharing corporate structures, of Baron Karl Vogelsang, first in Germany and later in Austria where he edited the Catholic newspaper *Vaterland*, and particularly of Giuseppe Toniolo in Italy, were all studied by De Gasperi and he saw their thoughts reflected in Leo XIII's great encyclical, *Rerum Novarum*, published on May 18th, 1901. De Gasperi had been a great student of the thoughts and teachings of these men, and had been as deeply influenced, (as were Schuman and Adenauer) by the advocates of social justice and opponents of Marxist class-war.

[1] *I. Cattolici Dall'Opposizione al Governo*, De Gasperi (Laterza, Bari, 1955).

De Gasperi early pointed out the dangers of the "convergence of nationalism and syndicalism". Enrico Corradini, as early as 1910, showed his revolutionary syndicalism, namely trade union organisation combining with "heroic nationalism". De Gasperi stated clearly that this "heroic nationalism" "contained the same scale of virtue, will and energy, the same moral origins and hence the same morality, as Fascism and Communism".

Georges Valois, the French nationalist and union leader, supported both the corporate teachings of Count de la Tour du Pin and of the Socialist Henri Sorel, and published his best-selling *Economie Nouvelle* (New Economy) on the ideas of integral syndicalism in 1919. In it he advocated that all economic matters should be removed from Parliament and regulated for the State by an economic "social council elected from all the working professions". De Gasperi pointed out that Valois did not realise that this obviously gave the State full control.

Remedies were needed for the always more destructive class struggle, a threat before the First World War which reappeared after World War II. The Marxist solution of a classless state established by the dictatorship of the proletariat was popular with a growing section of society. It received a special impetus from former liberals among the professionals and academicians who were now embracing the materialist dialectics of Marxism.

In his writings De Gasperi took issue with the Marxist view, which abolished class by destruction, advocating instead the unifying Christian principle of the brotherhood of man, based on the common fatherhood of God. Here De Gasperi represented precisely the same school of thought as Adenauer and Schuman.

But all three early saw a danger of misinterpretation even of the Christian concept of brotherhood. A strange amalgam of Christian social teachings and Marxist materialistic objectives appeared as a precursor of the totalitarian State, a community so structured as to eliminate all individual political expression. All individuals were arranged in groups, Corporations, Fasci, Staende, Guilds or Unions ruled in their turn by one single overriding authority which set the rules for each—and there we have the totalitarian State. Thus in the last analysis there was a political affinity between all totalitarian States in practice, whether Communist, Fascist, Corporative, National Socialist or just Socialist. To them, all were but units expressing the collective consent.

It was the corporate classless state which appealed most strongly to the once devout Marxist, Benito Mussolini, as it did to many of Hitler's theoreticians.

De Gasperi wrote years later that by 1921 the Fascist programme included integrated corporatism. Mussolini advocated Fascist corporations, unions of entire professions rather than associations of employees and employers separately. Thirteen years later, in 1934, the Fascist state passed a law, authorising the Head of State to constitute "integral corporations" for many "large sections of production". Similar ideas, borrowing their phraseology from Catholic social teachings, but denuded of their Christian context, could also be found in the writings of the Austrian Otmar Spann, *Der Wahre Staat*, which virtually became the bible of the theoreticians of national-socialism. The Soviet version of the integrated totalitarian state merely substituted for the word *Staende* or *Fasci* (professions or industry) the Soviet state unions. From farmers to industrial workers, including the respective professions belonging to those areas of production, such as engineers and other scientists, all were organised, but organised under and for the State.

There were special problems inherent in the transition of the largely agricultural and hierarchically structured society of pre-1914 Europe into the urban industrial age of mass production when the individual artisan rapidly became man-in-the-mass. In the closely structured and historically conscious societies of the Old World, there was an added problem. The purely economic and social changes raised the question of how to replace the earlier traditional forms of authority of local landlords, how to substitute administrative functions of the aristocracy with those of the bureaucracy of a democratic regime, which was not yet endowed with the same acceptance or deference in the eyes of the people. Traditional forms of authority were often strictly circumscribed because they were divided between several sources of authority, like local customs, spiritual or feudal loyalties.

The democratic regime established its single authority based primarily on majority votes. In many of the countries we have seen this transition ending in autocratic power being bestowed on dictators. These powers were far in excess of what any aristocratically structured society ever could claim for its rulers, who had been not only privileged, but also strictly limited in their rights by feudal tradition. New rulers, like Stalin or Hitler, were not restrained by the imperative traditions which limited even a "divine ruler" like a Mikado or an Emperor "by the Grace of God".

After World War II there was one overriding threat to the sound restoration of institutions of political life in the various war-torn countries. The founding of the German Empire in 1871 and the founding of the Kingdom of Italy a few years earlier, had already shown up the danger of exaggerating the advantages of merging all individual interests in an allegedly royal or imperial or, for that matter, republican State. The word "state" took on an almost magic connotation for people at the urging of their leaders, who had assumed the role of founding fathers. This completely obscured another basic fact. This fact is that there is no such a reality as a "state" except to the extent to which a group of people, or a single person, but always individual human beings, act as or for the State. Unfortunately, this very concept of a State as an impersonal abstraction arbitrating between allegedly antagonistic individual interests appeals to many sections of society, not excluding some Catholics. A number of the latter even managed to read into *Rerum Novarum* and *Quadragesimo Anno* their own pet concept of the state as an overriding power. This was one of De Gasperi's serious pre-occupations when he undertook his great work of reconstruction after World War II, as it had been when he was involved in the political life of the old Austro-Hungarian Empire.

He was pre-occupied with the breakdown of parliamentary democracy, which had occurred periodically and in various countries from the very beginning of the century. De Gasperi found that the difficulty of making democracy work in countries like France, for example, had deep roots. France had had its own organic constituent existence. Many regional district and individual loyalties were destroyed by centralising concentration of power in the hands of a few, namely a centrally directed bureaucracy, ruling from above, from Paris. In England the House of Commons had remained at all times a representative body, representing regions caused by the existence of geographic rather than numerical constituencies. In a way the proportional representation system of France's Third Republic and of the German Weimar Republic disenfranchised traditional safeguards, which retained sufficient influence for men who were closely linked to their own home counties to limit centralised power. These French difficulties prevailed long after the period studied by De Gasperi and were very recently vividly illustrated by the almost authoritarian rule of General de Gaulle in the Fifth Republic.

In another analysis De Gasperi showed that the radically centralising Treaty of Versailles destroyed the German federation of kingdoms, dukedoms, principalities and sovereign free privileged cities, like Cologne, and completed Bismarck's efforts for a "unified" German state. As a result, the survival of parliamentary democracy in Germany became questionable. The state which Bismarck created, and even less the state created by the Versailles Treaty, had not emerged as a cohesive organic federal unit. Organically independent units, with their own characteristics, were being submerged by an imposed uniformity. De Gasperi believed that with the destruction of local autonomies, (true federalism) parliamentary democracy is doomed. At best it can only function well in a very small and homogeneous state. He believed that in modern times no people accept centralised bureaucratic control for long from bodies which have no affinities with people's more intimate neighbourhood and environmental problems. Parliament must be truly representative—not merely as an arithmetic nose count for voting purposes—or it becomes a rule from above, a rule of the people rather than a rule by the people.

The economic crisis of the Thirties had shown that the liberally oriented economy, largely based on laissez-faire theories of absolute property rights, could not survive.

De Gasperi urged all Catholics and non-Catholics to study the Papal pronouncements more carefully. He referred specially to *Quadragesimo Anno* and noticed that it had five main points dealing with the social order and with associations, also called corporations. From the first to the last point each concrete outline is predicated on free choice by the individual, on personal liberty and on respect for human dignity. De Gasperi stressed that it must not be overlooked that the Pope demanded at all times that all organisations must be based on justice and charity and full respect for the individual.

"Hence when we talk of a corporate state in *Quadragesimo Anno*", De Gasperi wrote, "we are dealing with social and economic matters, not with political systems . . . The Church does not involve itself in affairs of State but deals with directions on basic principles. As far as *Quadragesimo Anno* and before it, *Rerum Novarum*, envisaged the establishment of associations, these are only seen as being grafted onto the healthy structure of a Christian state. Thus every political system or practical application of principles must first of all be judged in the light of such an ideal (Christian) state. What is too often overlooked in trying to apply certain suggestions regarding the social order which are contained in the Papal teachings, is that charity and justice are the principal directives, unalterable in all circumstances, while methods, whether associations or corporations or unions or other organisms formed for practical purposes, must vary with individual circumstances."[1]

De Gasperi was insistent in pointing out how in *Divini Redemptoris* the section dealing with atheistic Communism was being politically exploited by certain anti-Communist political regimes who were giving the silent treatment to the equally important section in which the Pope specifies the abuses and the injustices in the existing social and economic order of Western society which paved the way for atheistic Communism. De Gasperi underlined also that the Pope

[1] *I. Cattolici Dall' Opposizione al Governo*, De Gasperi (Laterza, Bari, 1955).

proposed remedies to counteract, not just to combat the political system of Communism. He took issue with the liberal teachings of economic society by stating that the fundamental difference between them and the Christian doctrine is that there are other and more binding obligations and rights than merely those incorporated in a work contract.

When we, therefore, take the two salient points underlined by the Church, namely the threat to individual freedom by claims of national states to assume unrestricted economic responsibilities and the sole right of the state to define the social and political obligations of the individual, it is not difficult to see how three devoted Catholics and dedicated patriots were early involved in political opposition to their nationalistic and centralising governments. It is against this background that the subsequent and decisive roles played by De Gasperi in Italy, Konrad Adenauer in Germany and Robert Schuman in France, and above all, by all three in a post-World War II reconstituted Free World, will be more readily understood.

CHAPTER IV

A Strange Interlude

To all three men World War I marked a turning point of decisive importance for their political future. For Schuman and De Gasperi it meant the political incorporation of their homeland into their cultural "mother country". Alsace-Lorraine, which till then Schuman had known only as a Prussian province, became part of France, and in 1919 Schuman entered politics as a Deputy of the French Assembly.

For De Gasperi the end of the war meant a basic reorientation of his political future. From a stalwart defender of minority rights and interests of the Italians of the Trentino, Friuli and Istria against the strong pro-German ruling groups of the Habsburg monarchy, both at court and in parliament, De Gasperi, for a few years only, found himself a member of the Italian Parliament. But again we see him defending his homeland. This time it is against the social and religious encroachments of a secularistic and centralising Italian majority in a parliament itself in mortal combat against the rise of Fascism.

Of the three men, only Konrad Adenauer remained within the same national state. But that state lay in economic ruins, had to face the consequences of military defeat and emerged as a temporary republic which was lack-lustre and divided as to its very political nature.

The end of World War I had ushered all three men into positions where the struggle for universal principles, hitherto defended primarily in relationship to the immediate surroundings of an integrated homeland, extended into a wider national and international field. Their profound religious convictions, their deep-rooted democratic traditions and fervent attachment to the welfare of their people, were to be tested in the crucible of political polemics transcending local boundaries and at white heat. For each of them, their religious and political attachments soon involved personal sufferings, imprisonments and the life of the fugitive, each being pursued by the law officers of his own countrymen. This marked them deeply also for the world role each was to assume at the end of another world war.

Konrad Adenauer had been moving up in the civic administration of Cologne when war broke out between France and Germany in August 1914. His difficult task of organising food supplies and war-time economic measures was complicated by the problem of large concentrations of troops in this Western German fortress and garrison town, which became a staging point and supply base for the nearby battle-line in Flanders and later the great battles around Verdun and the Marne.

But his official preoccupations were more than matched by a series of domestic concerns. After the birth of three children, Emma Adenauer died on October 10th, 1916. There followed sad and difficult years for Adenauer, who had been deeply attached to his wife. She had been a source of inspiration, understanding and encouragement in his political struggle and achievements.

Some months after his wife's death, Konrad Adenauer was involved in a serious car accident. Apparently the chauffeur of the official car fell asleep, or lost control, and crashed into a tram. Adenauer, sitting in the back seat, was thrown through the glass into the street. Despite severe injuries, bleeding profusely from head wounds, with broken cheekbones and a broken lower jaw, he walked to the nearby hospital. For a while there was fear for his eye-sight, the injury having affected the position of his eyes, resulting in double vision.

This is how an eye-witness described the accident to his eldest son, Koko (Konrad): "The car was just a mass of twisted metal. I would never have believed that even a mouse could have been alive in the wreckage. Then, slowly, a man came crawling out from under it, straightened himself up and, streaming with blood, walked away, stiff as a poker. That was Herr Adenauer. The driver was only slightly injured, but he had himself carried away on a stretcher."[1] The surgeon had to stitch the wounds without an anaesthetic due to the loss of blood. After the operation was over, Adenauer fainted and remained unconscious for some time. It was this accident which so changed his appearance that he was not infrequently described by the press as "That old Indian Chief".

While he was still recuperating in the nursing home the position of Lord Mayor fell vacant, Max Wallraf the incumbent Lord Mayor having accepted a Cabinet post in Berlin. Konrad Adenauer was installed as Wallraf's successor on October 18th, 1917 at the age of forty-one. He had obtained thirty-five out of a total of thirty-seven

[1] *Konrad Adenauer*, Paul Weymar (André Deutsch, London, 1957).

votes. The voting system of the City Council was based on the Three Estates principle, the largest property owners, with multiple votes based on the size of their property, dominating the Liberal Party. Here the Wallrafs ruled as "substantial citizens" and had a decisive influence, which they were willing to throw behind Adenauer's candidature, perhaps partly because his late wife's mother was a Wallraf. The Second Estate of Medium Proprietors as well as the single vote proprietors of the Third Estate gave the Catholic Centre Party its strength. That party had long looked upon Konrad Adenauer as a special candidate and leading light in their party council. Thus at the end of the war, as Lord Mayor of the ancient city of Cologne, he exercised exceptional political power in the country, since by virtue of his new position as Lord Mayor of Cologne, he also had a seat in the Upper Chamber of the Prussian Legislature of which he was eventually to become president.

As the war clouds over Germany began to darken, Adenauer realised that great changes were impending. By early 1918 he seemed to foresee clearly that Germany had lost the war and doubted that the monarchy would survive defeat. With the first cracks in Germany's Western defences, Cologne began to feel the brunt of the retreating armies.

One of the more painful notes in Adenauer's memoirs from those days seems to have been the utter collapse of military discipline, not so much of the troops themselves as of the higher command. Apparently the General in charge of the Cologne military district completely lost his nerve, yielding to rioters and extremists, despite Adenauer's efforts and resolution to maintain law and order and defend the Cologne citizenry from looting and marauding troops in retreat.

It was only with the arrival of a new military commander, the Bavarian Captain Otto Schwink, who possessed considerable courage, that Adenauer found a man with whom he could co-operate. Their united courage would not have been sufficient, however, had it not been coupled with Adenauer's ability to negotiate with the revolutionary committees, whom he managed to get round a conference table. Thus it was possible to maintain comparative calm with a minimum of discipline, preventing the disruption of services and supplies during the critical days when German regiments were either being disbanded in Cologne itself, or marched through to the rear. Three days after the last regiments, still in orderly formation, had retreated through Cologne, the British army entered the city.

The new British Commander handed the Lord Mayor a printed British proclamation to be posted throughout the city. Apart from the usual orders regarding curfew, traffic circulation and assembly, there was one paragraph, namely Paragraph 13, ordering "male German civilians to demonstrate their respect for British officers by doffing their hats on passing". Adenauer doubtless recalled a similar order handed to the Swiss by the Austrian Governor Gessler several centuries earlier. The defiance of this order by the Swiss culminated in the condemnation of William Tell, the Swiss patriot, to shoot an apple placed on the head of his son. After slowly reading Paragraph 13, Adenauer turned to the British Staff Officer who had brought him the order, and is reported as saying that he could not believe "that an English gentleman would want to humiliate a vanquished people in this manner". The General's reply was that his orders merely stipulated that he should hand Adenauer the proclamation. It was Adenauer's responsibility what he did with it. Thereupon Adenauer picked up the parcel and placed it in the corner of his room, where it remained. The British never enquired why the proclamation was not posted.

It was indicative of Adenauer's constant concern for the future that in the midst of all the misery and critical food shortages, aggravated by thousands of refugees seeking help in the metropolis, he turned the dismantling of the fortress belt around Cologne (under British military orders) into one of the most important urban improvements. He decided to use the fortress belt around the city for a re-forestation project which became the famous "green belt" of Cologne, since imitated by many other cities.

It is striking to compare the relations established between the Lord Mayor of Cologne, Konrad Adenauer and the British Military Commander Sir Sidney Clive in 1919 and between Adenauer (still Lord Mayor) and Brigadier Barraclough the British Commander in 1945. While General Clive derived much benefit not only for the inhabitants but also for British policy from Adenauer's administrative ability and wisdom, Brigadier Barraclough escalated incivility to the point of fining him and placing him under a political ban. Sir Sidney Clive was political adviser to the Commander-in-Chief and was stationed in Cologne as Military Commander of the British occupied Rhineland. General Clive and Konrad Adenauer established an extremely useful relationship, based on mutual confidence and respect.

Even more significant was the close co-operation between Adenauer and the British Commander on the question of Rhineland's separatist movement, promoted by France and opposed by the British, which flared up immediately after the German defeat in 1918. Designed to detach the Rhineland from Germany, the movement was led by Dr. Dorten, a lawyer from Wiesbaden, who was strongly backed by French funds and French political pressure in Allied councils. Dorten approached Adenauer as the Lord Mayor of Cologne and the key figure in the Rhineland. The object was not only to detach the Rhineland from Prussia, which had administered it as a province since 1815, but also to detach it from the German state. While the Rhineland's incorporation into the East German Prussian kingdom of the Hohenzollerns was never too popular with many a Western oriented Rhinelander, a detachment from *Germany* was definitely regarded as treasonable. This was amply demonstrated by Adenauer's subsequent moves which are of interest here as a background to some of the problems he was to experience with the Nazis in later years. It soon became apparent to Adenauer that the movement of Dr. Dorten had a powerful backer in Georges Clemenceau, the "tiger" of France, while British policy was more than unsympathetic, if not militantly hostile, to the French ambitions. Because of the British desire not to show their own hostility to the French by openly challenging Dorten's activities, Adenauer decided to play for time. Patience was always one of his political strong points.

To everybody's surprise, Adenauer invited Rhineland political leaders to meet at the Cologne City Hall on February 1st, 1919 to discuss the future of the Rhineland. He even indicated a possibility of establishing a new West-German state. Dorten's separatist group came to the meeting, advocating outright separation of such a state from Germany. The others looked upon a West German state merely as an autonomous province (Land) within a German federation. It was here that Adenauer showed his political finesse. As Chairman, he did not have to declare himself and nobody knew exactly where he stood, thus enabling him to deal with both groups and between both groups. At the end of the session, at which he gave a political exposé lasting three and a half hours, he achieved a unanimous resolution which protested against "all plans and efforts, now discernible in the press and foreign countries, aiming at the detachment of the left bank of the Rhine, or part of it, from Germany", while at the same time expressing willingness to work on plans for a West-German republic within the framework of the German Reich. The Chairman of the study committee to work on such plans was again Konrad Adenauer, elected unanimously. In this some saw Adenauer emerging as the new head of the Rhineland separatists. In fact, he killed the movement since he never convened the study committee of which he had been elected Chairman. He went even further. When Sir Sidney Clive, upset by the news reaching him, taxed Adenauer that he had gone back on his earlier assurances not to support separatism and asked what the Mayor thought his next move should be, Adenauer tendered his advice.

He drafted a decree for the British Military Governor, which the latter accepted, that prohibited any constitutional changes in the Rhineland. This decree was immediately posted all over the British Zone and Dr. Dorten's movement collapsed. A "revolutionary tribunal" of Dr. Dorten's followers, who apparently recognised the author of this decree, expressed its profound resentment of Adenauer's tactics and passed a sentence of death *in absentia* on Konrad Adenauer. In his memoirs, *Grandeurs et Misères d'une Victoire*, Georges Clemenceau laments that his plans to detach the Rhineland were thwarted by the Lord Mayor of Cologne.[1]

But Adenauer had one more battle to fight against separatism, and this time not against France. The separatist appeared, curiously enough, in the person of no less a German statesman than Gustav Stresemann, at that particular time Chancellor, although better known as Foreign Minister, a position he held in subsequent Cabinets. Stresemann was supported by his Finance Minister Hans Luther.

It will be remembered that France had insisted on re-occupying the industrial Ruhr basin and held the Rhineland captive against defaulted reparation payments which she knew Germany could not pay. This occurred after the Versailles Treaty had been signed and military forces of the Allies had been withdrawn. Germany strained to maintain an artificial life in those areas the French had occupied as assurance against payment of these reparations. Germany was pouring in subsidies for welfare and unemployment relief which she could ill afford. A galloping inflation had been braked, but only braked by the introduction of a fiat currency by Hjalmar Schacht, the then Reich currency commissar. He had conceived what was called the "*Rentenmark*", but the drain of subsidising the French occupied Ruhr, whose vital economy was paralysed, threatened the new currency.

On November 13th, 1923 representatives of the Rhineland population were summoned to Berlin to meet with Reichskanzler Gustav Stresemann. According to Adenauer's own account, "the Rhinelanders were horrified" when Stresemann told them that they should separate from the Reich by the establishment of a separate Rheinish state. "You ask Mr. Tirard, the President of the Inter-Allied Commission at Koblenz tomorrow! You must ask him to grant you the right to levy your own taxes in the occupied territories. And then you will just have to see how you get along", Stresemann is quoted in Adenauer's notes of this meeting. Dr. Hans Luther, then Finance Minister, supported Stresemann as did Dr. Otto Braun, the

[1] *Grandeur and Misery of Victory*, English translation (Harrap, London, 1930).

Socialist Premier of Prussia. When Adenauer asked Dr. Braun how he could even contemplate amputating two provinces, for which he was responsible, from Prussia, the Socialist Premier just shrugged his shoulders. The argument continued with rising acrimony for several hours and ended only when Stresemann suddenly slumped in his chair, suffering a heart attack, one of the early ones in a series which culminated in his death a number of years later. The attitude of the Rhinelanders was, "If the Government can muster the sad courage to surrender and sacrifice part of Germany, then let them stand up themselves with their plans before the German people". Adenauer adds, "We know that no government would dare to take such a step", and the Rhinelanders certainly were not going to be used by the Central Government to assume this responsibility before history.

Shortly thereafter the Stresemann government resigned and Dr. Wilhelm Marx formed a new one. To Adenauer's great surprise the group of Rhinelanders were again summoned, this time by the new Chancellor, "to continue the discussion". Adenauer first insisted on having the Finance Minister Hans Luther present at the meeting, and then proceeded to demolish the financial analysis which Marx had received from Luther. Marx finally admitted that there seemed to be another aspect to the question and the entire plan was dropped, with Adenauer emerging for the second time as the successful champion against separatism.

What must have been Adenauer's thoughts when, twenty-three years later, he again faced a situation summed up in a dispatch I read during my first post-war visit to Europe. On May 23rd, 1946 the following dispatch sent from Cologne by John Elliot to the *New York Herald*, said:

"All the big political parties are definitely committed to the idea of a united Germany. They are afraid of a hitherto obscure Rhinelander who has started a mass movement to separate the Rhineland from the Reich.

"Dr. Fritz Opitz, thirty-five year old leader of the Rheinische Volks Partei, is feared by the Communists, Socialists, Democrats and the Christian Democratic Union, because his party, with headquarters here, has the avowed objective of setting up a Rhine republic. 'An independent Rhineland is the only guarantee of peace', Opitz told me yesterday. 'History has shown over and over again that a strong Germany, dominated by Russia, means a war of expansion'.

"Dr. Konrad Adenauer, who is really the outstanding political leader in the Rhineland, admitted he was uneasy over the political potentiality of the upstart movement. Adenauer said that the Rhinelanders did not want to tear themselves loose from Germany, but their despair and frustration, born of the present seemingly hopeless situation, might persuade them to seek a way out in such a solution.

"The Rheinische Volks Partei has branches throughout the Rhineland in both the British and the French Zones, twenty-seven in the former and six in the latter. Opitz said he already has 80,000 paying members in his party, which was founded last June. The party demands an immediate plebiscite on the independence of the Rhineland and Opitz asserts that if a plebiscite were held today, the party could get 78–80 per cent of the votes."

Obviously, the most important paying member of the Opitz party was France. The emergence of a political structure under Adenauer's leadership, culminating in the establishment of a German government under him, relegated Dr. Opitz, like his predecessor Dr. Dorten and the Saar separatists after both world wars, to the collection of similar failures of French initiative. Doubtless these failures also led France to realise eventually that a more positive and lasting solution to their problem lay along a road of understanding and mutual co-operation. It was on that course that Robert Schuman was to embark her later.

* * *

The years of World War I were particularly difficult for the German citizen Robert Schuman, a practising lawyer in Metz, fortunately exempted from military service in the German army, fervently French in his sympathies, suffering for the hardship that war brought to his borderland people in what to many of them seemed fratricidal warfare, and not infrequently suspected by both sides. In order to mobilise Schuman into the war effort, he was assigned to work in a munition arsenal at the beginning of the war. He was later transferred to government service in the financial section of the administration of Bouley. He devoted all his spare time to assisting refugees or prisoners, making particular use of his Catholic contacts for charitable efforts, which sometimes had to cross the combat lines.

It was when the German military power collapsed and Alsace-Lorraine was occupied by French troops, that Schuman was forced into assuming a larger political role. The *Volksverein*, of which he had been a member, had to reconstitute itself into a political party, seeking representation in the French Chamber. In 1918 Schuman's friends urged upon him that his duty lay in presenting himself as a candidate. It was his friend Canon Collin who asked, "What do you do about your aspirations to defend social justice and the Church? Are you forgetting the parable of the talents? It prohibits your taking refuge in the structures of your province". Finally Schuman acceded to these entreaties and permitted his name to be put forward for nomination. He became a candidate on the list of the *Union Republicaine Lorraine* and in the elections of October 19th, 1919, he received 96 out of 116 party votes. On November 16th of that year he was elected as one of the seven members of his party and they made a triumphal entry into the French Chamber at the Palais Bourbon on December 9th, 1919. Even Clemenceau, always so suspicious of the "border folk", greeted them in warm terms, as did all other members of the French Chamber, except the Socialists. Albert Thomas, the Socialist, immediately challenged the right to Catholic education and attacked the new members on these fundamental issues which even the Germans had not dared to attack during their years of rule over Alsace-Lorraine. Once the enthusiasm over the re-incorporation of Alsace-Lorraine had given place to the ordinary approach to the traditional problems of French politics, Schuman found himself very rapidly involved in a difficult struggle for the maintenance of local rights and traditional privileges. Reunion with a political fatherland had been achieved but the problems of his own homeland began to loom large.

* * *

Of the three, it was Alcide De Gasperi who, in the years immediately after the first world war and the subsequent struggle which culminated in the political integration of his homeland into Italy, suffered some of the harshest experiences.

As long as Empires, kingdoms or other hereditary sovereignties existed nationalities were clearly defined entities, component parts of but not necessarily synonymous with that sovereignty. The sovereignty continued to exist frequently losing one or the other nationality under its rule, or adding others. Nationalities had developed out of more ancient, tribal cohesions, often at first based on language, religion, culture (when it emerged) and hereditary characteristics which were more or less stabilised through biological (genetic) factors or environmental similarities of climate, and through common experiences in defence against nature or other men, recorded as their history.

But as larger groups with common purposes, namely political ambitions, emerged which transcended tribal cohesions, a distinction had to be made between the nationality of a people and their status as citizens or as subjects within a larger political group. Thus when St. Paul proudly proclaimed that he was a Roman citizen (civis romanus sum) he certainly did not mean that he was a Roman, or as we would say to-day an Italian, and ceased to be a proud Jew of Tarsus, the nation to which he belonged.

Similarly in the days of the Holy Roman Empire of Charles V his political sovereignty, often loosely asserted, included Castilians and Germans, Italians—except those owing allegiance to the Papal States—Swiss, Bohemians and many more. Nothing in their relationship to the empire altered their also belonging to their particular and different nationality.

The 19th century aberration of equating state to nation, confusing citizenship with nationality, was shown up in all its absurdity by empires like the Austro-Hungarian, the Russian Empire and the Hohenzollern Germany of 1914. This absurdity contributed in no small measure to their individual downfalls. It was when pan-Slavism in Russia tried to make Slavs of Germans, Poles, Tartars, Georgians and the fifty or so other nationalities which made up the Empire of the Tsars, that they jeopardised the loyalty of hitherto good citizens and aroused separatism. This is what happened to Hohenzollern Germany with the Polish, Alsatian or Lorrainian citizens and to the Austria of the Hapsburgs when germanisation of Italians, Hungarians, Poles, Bohemians and South Slavs led to the break-up of the Danubian Empire-State.

The culminating foolishness of such confusion was years later when Adolf Hitler proclaimed a pure race principle as the basis of a state he called the Third Reich, hoping to have this myth turn into a mystique for what was probably one of the most racially mixed sections of the European peoples—namely the Germans of that Reich.

It was this modern nationalism, (a state policy of enforced uniformity created by artificial emotions in turn made possible only by a defensive appeal against an enemy) which proved so disruptive to Austria. It contradicted the very motto of Austria, namely *Bella gerunt alii—et tu felix Austria nubi* (Wars are fought by others, but you fortunate Austria marry). Through Habsburg marriages with the Medicis, the Estes, the Gonzagas and others, the territories of the Veneto, of the Trentino and even parts of Tuscany and Lombardy became rich heirlooms of the Habsburg family. Additional areas had become Austrian after the Congress of Vienna, following the defeat of Napoleon in 1815.

At the time Austria acquired her Italian minorities, there was no modern Italian state. Italy as a state only dates from 1861. Thus Italian nationality long predates Italian statehood, and was a much wider and more lasting concept.

The distinction between nationality and statehood cannot be stressed enough today when a certain bureaucratic over-simplification has invaded even the history classrooms. Doubtless the immigration laws of the New World have created, perhaps intentionally, an unwarranted confusion in defining people's nationalities, by equating nation and state. If a person is born in Russia, he is a Russian, even if merely a citizen of the Russian state, maybe by conquest, speaking German or Polish, Lithuanian or Tungus, according to his or her nationality. The desire of the United States, and to a certain extent of all the "immigrant" countries of the Western hemisphere, to fuse all nationalities artificially into a homogeneous population of "Americans" or "Canadians" or "Argentinos" or "Brazileros" etc. has generated a strong opposition to the teaching of history, even in the classrooms.

The reason for this, overt or covert, lies in the fear that history is divisive and tradition disruptive. Make people forget their different pasts and they will all merge into a united future. This policy of political "behaviourism" as a means of artificially creating nations out of states has taken a murderous toll of cultural acquisitions through the centuries and has become one of the most wasteful demographic heresies in which materially wealthy societies can engage. Many social problems, from broken homes and juvenile delinquency to race riots and separatist movements, are not unrelated to the sacrificing of national cultures and the uprooting of the traditions of a people. Instead of using different nationalities to create a rich and durable union, a human society endowed with all the worthy cultural acquisitions of the past, which is ready and strengthened by unity in diversity to face a peaceful common future, there emerges an uprooted mass of which no individual really or deeply feels an organic part. Sociologists would do well to seek some of the causes of the so-called alienations of the young (as well as of the old) here.

The struggle of the Italian minority in Austria, together with the difficulties experienced by other minorities of Slav origin when war broke out, was but a chapter in the history of the difficulties of the minorities in practically all the belligerent countries in 1914 and again when war broke out in 1939. All had larger or smaller ethnic groups belonging to the national majorities in enemy countries. Such situations had existed throughout the history of Europe and of other continents. They had never really presented a problem as long as nobody tried to equate sovereignty and nationality. When this modern concept appeared in the nineteenth and particularly in the early twentieth century, it was basically incapable of reasonable application in the modern sovereign state, because of the extremely heterogeneous composition of its people. Even the British royal family changed its surname from the German Guelphs (Hanover) to Windsor and the Battenbergs became Mountbatten, a camouflage which was insufficient at the time to permit Admiral Lord Mountbatten to assume his rightful rank in the British Navy. During the wars of our century, it has led to grave and sometimes most cruel injustices towards loyal citizens persecuted for their ethnic origins, whether they were Volga Germans in Russia, Greeks under Turkish rule, Japanese in British Columbia or California, Jews in Arab countries, Arabs in Palestine or Italians of the Trentino.

In the Trentino, even the Prince Archbishop of Trent, Mgr. Endrici, who had been the teacher and friend of De Gasperi from his student days, was removed from his See by the Most Catholic Emperor of Austria and put under house arrest in a monastery near Vienna: this because although he was an Austrian citizen he was of Italian nationality. A period of intense suffering began for De Gasperi's people—and for himself a period of heroic effort to alleviate their distress. He had to expose himself to reprisals and dangers of arrest every day. He went to Vienna, where his parliamentary immunity gave him greater protection than in his home province. Martial law had been declared there and the regime was under military command. In Vienna he devoted himself to mobilising material aid in the form of food and clothing for the thousands of Italians who had been arrested and transported for internment to concentration camps, in the interior of Austria, which had been hastily and therefore inadequately organised. He importuned the authorities, pleading for the mitigation of some of the dire hardships in these camps. The constant threat of the dissolution of the prorogued parliament hung over him and this would have meant the loss of his parliamentary immunity and immediate arrest. Other deputies from the Trentino, like Conci and Carlo De Bellat, had been arrested and confined by the Innsbruck local governor, because they refused to sign a declaration of fealty to Austria which he had edited in such a way that it also contained a bitter attack against everything Italian. De Gasperi also had refused to sign the declaration, but removed himself to the capital where the military and police authorities respected his parliamentary immunity. The plight of civilian camps having been brought to public attention by men like De Gasperi, a committee was established under the presidency of Baron Vladimir von Bech, who in turn acquired De Gasperi's services. With the backing of Baron von Bech, De Gasperi was able to visit the camps, particularly some of the worst like Braunau in Upper Austria, the birthplace of Adolf Hitler.

On the death of Emperor Francis Joseph, November 21st, 1916, Charles I ascended the throne as the last Emperor of Austria-Hungary. His first act was to dismiss the arch-nationalist Prime Minister Koerber and to appoint the moderate and progressive Count Heinrich Clam-Martinitz. Charles I also convoked Parliament for May 30th, 1917 after a prorogation which had lasted about three years. Austria's military situation eased when Russia defected from the Allied ranks because it was in the throes of a revolution, which had broken out in February 1917.

Despite the histrionic attempt of Alexander Kerensky, the socialist premier of the new Russian state, to rally the army for battle against the Germans, this proved impossible. Kerensky had destroyed the effectiveness of the Russian army by his famous Edict Number I which abolished all discipline for the soldiers, including the symbolic salute of privates to officers. Russia had ceased to be a military threat to the Central Powers. The German armies, relieved of Russian pressure in the East, were attacking France and actually bombarding the outskirts of Paris, and the Austrian Field-Marshal Konrad was massing troops in the Trentino against Italian forces. When Parliament met under Charles I in May 1917, there were seven Popolari from Trent, as Conci had also been released from internment by a special decree. But one Italian, the Socialist Battisti, also a representative from Trent, was missing. He had been hanged by the Austrian government on charges of high treason before the accession to the throne by Charles I.

All the ethnic groups, except the Poles and the Italians, made declarations in Parliament demanding reform of the Constitution, a reform which granted them local autonomy. Czech and Yugoslav minorities were particularly vociferous. The Poles, by that time hoping for a restoration of a free Poland which they wanted to join, reserved the right to speak at a later date. The Popolari of the Trentino refused to make any kind of declaration at the opening of parliament. But three weeks later, on June 22nd, 1917, De Gasperi made an interpellation which was acclaimed by all the ethnic groups and even the moderates of German Austria, as being nothing short of the heroic. He said he was not merely addressing himself to the government benches, but to the world in general when he denounced the plight of some 100,000 Italians from Trentino, from Friuli, from Istria and from Dalmatia. These people were detained in concentration camps under inhuman conditions, De Gasperi declared. He described all the horrors and persecutions to which they, including a great number of priests, many of whom had already died from their privations, were exposed. He brought up the scandal of the arrest of the Lord Archbishop of Trent, Celestino Endrici, who, despite his membership in the Upper House of Austria, had been denied his rights as a citizen of having his arrest justified before a court. De Gasperi attacked the unconstitutional arrest of a number of deputies. He demanded justice under law and protection by law for all citizens, even those of Italian or other nationalities. It caused a sensation when De Gasperi introduced an amendment to the motion on the budget, demanding that "the Imperial and Royal Government release all those citizens unjustly and illegally deprived of their liberty and recompense them for the economic losses and the damages sustained". More surprising even was that this amendment was passed almost unanimously on July 15th, 1917, with the vast majority of the German Austrians voting for it. This parliamentary relief measure was subsequently sabotaged by local governments who delayed the implementation of the law. De Gasperi again interpellated the Government, asking the Minister of the Interior whether he still considered himself competent to impose his own directives on military commanders who had defied his orders.

After a short summer recess, Parliament reconvened on September 25th, 1917. The political atmosphere had changed, events having played into the hands of the more chauvinistic nationalist elements. The Russian Socialist Alexander Kerensky was rapidly losing influence in Russia and his revolutionary government was being harassed by extremists. The Russian armies were rapidly disintegrating and had been routed in Galicia, on Austria's Eastern front. The Italian offensive under General Cadorna had bogged down and the Austrians were massing for a counter-attack which culminated in the utter rout of the Italian armies at Caporetto. The Germans were menacing Paris. However, De Gasperi again took the offensive, demanding the justice still denied to his people. He actually was able to mobilise essential support amongst other ethnic groups which proved strong enough to refuse to vote credits to the Government. But military success at the front had generated governmental euphoria, with Pan-German elements in the ascendency able to disregard the demands of ethnic minorities. Irritated by De Gasperi's obstruction, the Government felt strong enough at that point to threaten the dissolution of the House with the consequent arrest of De Gasperi, who would lose his immunity once the House was dissolved, and be no longer a member of Parliament.

However, De Gasperi's answer came on September 28th when he again denounced the separation of Archbishop Endrici from his See of Trent, lashing out at the Imperial Government by making odious comparisons between the persecution of the Church by the Bolsheviks who had assumed power in Russia and the actions of "Catholic Austria". "The revolutionary government of Russia has authorised the Archbishop of Leopoli (Lemberg) to return to his See, while Catholic Austria keeps a bishop away from his See because he has done what the Pope has asked him to do, namely admonished the faithful to hold to their sacred obligations". This was a reference to Archbishop Endrici's pastoral letter, urging special perseverance and particular devotion to the Sacred Heart, praying

Christ to intercede for the people now suffering. The Imperial Government read into the pastoral letter criticism of its own actions towards the victims in concentration camps. They had branded it as disloyal and had tried to suppress it. Actually, it had been De Gasperi who had brought out the pastoral letter from the Archbishop. Kept *incommunicado*, the Archbishop received only such privileged visits as a Member of Parliament such as De Gasperi could pay him. De Gasperi then organised the letter's distribution in the diocese.

"That zone (the Trentino), inhabited by some 300,000 people, is subjected to the terror of a number of bureaucrats who behave like miniature tyrants. They act probably in the spirit of the Prime Minister (Seidler, who had succeeded the more moderate Clam-Martinitz), who declares that it is necessary to leave these people to wallow in their own filth. Other officials have publicly introduced punishment by the lash", De Gasperi exclaimed to a tense House. "These tyrants think that because all is quiet, they are dealing with a cemetery. But let the spirit of freedom return and these dead bones will take on flesh, as once in the days of the Prophet, and they will be reassembled and shall return as live and free men. We can say with complete tranquillity in the words of the great German poet: 'Let the guilt of the tyrants increase, until that day comes in which the sins of the individual and the general evil will be atoned for together' ". As De Gasperi sat down after uttering these brave words of defiance, he was greeted from various benches with loud calls of Bravo! On October 23rd the credits came to a vote. Despite threats and intimidations, De Gasperi and his Popolari voted against the credits, and it was particularly noted that the basically anti-clerical liberal member from Trent, Baron Malfatti, voted with the Popolari. De Gasperi maintained his position to the very end. This end was not far off.

At first De Gasperi drew enough support from other groups to threaten the passage of the military credits. It was only after a personal intervention by the Emperor, asking for and receiving the Polish vote as well as that of the Italian Socialists from Trieste, who broke rank with the Italian group and voted with their fellow Socialists of Austria for the measure, that the passage of the credits was assured. Thereupon Parliament adjourned, and at least for a while De Gasperi lost his parliamentary platform from which he could fight for the rights of his people.

But De Gasperi missed no opportunity of exposing himself to the anger of the Government and to threats of reprisals. When Conci, a member of his party, made a biting speech in Prague before a group of Czechs on the occasion of the fiftieth anniversary of the Czech theatre, and a resolution was passed urging a common front amongst Czechs, Poles, Yugoslavs and Italians to co-operate in the revindication of minority rights, an effort was made to accuse Conci of anti-Austrian subversive actions as an individual. De Gasperi immediately made a public declaration, published in the Trieste newspaper, *Il Lavoratore di Trieste*, (May 15th, 1918), saying that Conci had not acted as an individual but had spoken for all members of the Popolari, indicating that any action taken against Conci should be taken against all other members of the party, an action which of course the Austrian Government did not dare to risk. De Gasperi declared that Conci's statement was but "the cry of desperation of the people whose very existence is threatened".

About that time De Gasperi again visited the Archbishop of Trent, who was still confined to a monastery near Vienna. This time they met secretly in the forest near the Abbey. At this clandestine meeting Archbishop Endrici entrusted to him a new pastoral letter to his people of the Trentino, in which he asked for special prayers and fortitude in the defence of liberty, and the preservation of the dignity of the teaching Church and of her ministers. The Archbishop also asked for special prayers on the feast of the Sacred Heart on June 7th, 1918. De Gasperi got the letter printed in the parish bulletins of the individual churches before the authorities were aware of it, and had them distributed on Pentecost Sunday, May 13th. The authorities tried to suppress further distribution of the pastoral letter, but it was too late. Despite all efforts to prevent such manifestations, the cathedral of Trent was packed on the feast day of the Sacred Heart and De Gasperi, Conci, Degentile and De Lugan, all members of Parliament, took part. Only eight days later, before repressive measures could be effected, the advance of the Austrian army bogged down.

On June 23rd, 1918 General Diaz launched an Italian offensive which ended with the rout of the Austrians at Vittorio Veneto. From then on events seemed to precipitate themselves. The Germans were stopped at the Marne. On September 29th, Bulgaria sued for an armistice; thus Austria's southern defences collapsed. A few days later the new Premier, Baron Hussarek, announced that Charles I had offered autonomy to the ethnic groups. The only audible comment heard in Parliament was an interruption which came from the German member Zenker, "Too late".

Then De Gasperi took the floor, and in an impassioned speech told Parliament that after what his people had suffered, after having been treated as enemies and denied protection as citizens, their hopes could henceforth be pinned only on the fortunes of the Italian people as a whole. He ended his speech with a significant quotation from

Dante: "We Italians must bow our heads; so must you foreigners. Let us raise our heads together, brothers in justice". While the Vienna Nationalist paper, *Reichspost*, bitterly attacked De Gasperi, at least it correctly described his speech as a "farewell to Austria".

When Parliament was reconvened on October 22nd, following a declaration by President Woodrow Wilson of the United States about the self-determination of peoples, Emperor Charles stated that he wished to turn Austria into a federated State. In this each nationality would enjoy self-determination within its own ethnic and geographical boundaries, but various deputies representing ethnic groups refused to co-operate. The Rumanians, the Ruthenians and the Czechs simply said that they already had representatives of their governments in Paris and no longer considered themselves part of Austria. The Yugoslavs made a similar declaration, and the people of the Trentino had already seven days previously informed the Austrian government that they considered themselves from now on part of their "mother country", Italy. On October 24th the Italian deputies in the Austrian Chamber, the Popolari and the Liberals together, without the Socialists, prepared a statement which Conci gave to the public. In it they stated that, basing their stand on the principles laid down by President Wilson, they solemnly declared that "all territories having an Italian population are no longer subject to the Austro-Hungarian monarchy, and therefore are entering into discussions with Italy. Hence, they will have no further discussions to continue with the Austrian Government". The statement went on to say that all territories inhabited by Italians within the Austro-Hungarian monarchy must therefore now be considered as belonging to the Italian State. But for this declaration to take practical effect, some time had to elapse.

The incorporation of the Trentino and other areas into the Italian state had to await the signature of the peace treaty of St. Germain, which meant that De Gasperi could not be a candidate in the election of 1919 in Italy because he had not yet obtained Italian citizenship. It was not until the election of 1921 that De Gasperi, now an Italian citizen, could present himself. Meantime he and Don Sturzo, the founder of the Popolari, the Catholic Party, were working on making its parliamentary group an active factor in the new Italian Parliament. De Gasperi was elected head of the party, while the Lombard Cavazzoni acted both as secretary and mentor on questions of Italian internal politics, with which the former Austrian member of Parliament was not familiar. De Gasperi's first impression of Rome and its parliamentary practices were rather negative, according to Giulio Andreotti.[1] "In the Viennese Parliament, even during some

[1] *De Gasperi e il Suo Tempo*, Giulio Andreotti (Mondadori, Milan).

of the bitterest debates, a certain form and dignity, even in attacks against political opponents, were respected. The manners of the members of the Italian Parliament on the Montecitorio seemed shocking to De Gasperi. On the Montecitorio it seemed to take only a petty issue to unleash personal insults and acrimonious exchanges. It did not take long for the trained parliamentarian De Gasperi to realise the gravity and the perils threatening the Italian political situation."

Benito Mussolini was not the least of the threats facing Italian parliamentary government: he entered Parliament in the same election as De Gasperi who had already crossed swords with him in the Trentino as far back as 1909. Mussolini had contested a seat in 1919 in the general election immediately after the cessation of hostilities, but unsuccessfully. By 1921 the political crisis in Italy brought the Fascists to the fore and Mussolini into Parliament: thus De Gasperi's joining the Italian people was not merely the achievement of a goal, but the beginning of a bitter and dangerous struggle for freedom and religious liberty, as well as for democratic government. It was to become a struggle which was sometimes even more bitter and certainly more cruel than that which he had experienced in his days as a member of the Austro-Hungarian Parliament.

Chapter V

The Twilight Years of Peace

In the period after the first world war Europe saw the emergence of Adenauer, De Gasperi and Schuman as national legislators. They were no longer the defenders of the somewhat circumscribed interests of towns or minorities within a wider, often hostile, Sovereign State.

Adenauer, Lord Mayor of Cologne, had played an active part in all German affairs when he became the opponent of Rhineland separatism and assumed a leading role in the councils of the Zentrum party as well as in the Prussian Upper House.

Robert Schuman was now not only a member of the newly incorporated Alsace-Lorraine group of deputies at the Palais Bourbon, but a French parliamentarian, responsible for French policy.

Alcide De Gasperi emerged as the Head of an all-Italian party, the *Popolari*, in an Italian parliament, with the fate of Italian parliamentary government as one of his major concerns. His parliamentary career between the two wars was to be very brief, and the "liberation" of his homeland most deceptive in terms of freedom.

Soon after his election to the Italian parliament in 1921, De Gasperi went to Germany in company with Don Sturzo, the founder and inspirer of the *Popolari* movement, in order to meet representatives of Germany's Catholic party, the *Zentrum*, of which Konrad Adenauer was also a member. They were anxious to establish international bonds of co-operation along similar social and political lines, namely those of a Christian democracy. These efforts to work on a wider European scale beyond the confines of a narrow nationalism, were quickly cut short. In Italy it was not long before the narrowest form of aggressive nationalism assumed power under Mussolini.

De Gasperi was soon fully preoccupied with Italian politics. He had to face the antagonism of the Socialists who, as avowed Marxist materialists, saw in a social doctrine taught under Christian auspices a danger to their highly developed ideological class warfare. He also incurred the equally bitter enmity of the anti-clerical bourgeoisie represented by the Liberal party of the then Prime Minister,

Francesco Saverio Nitti. But at least these battles were still being fought under the general consensus of democratic parliamentary procedures.

But while the democratic parties were fighting among themselves, incapable of forming a stable government and continually indulging in sterile intrigues of voting combines in the struggle for position, power and sometimes mere material profit, the figure of Mussolini with his rapidly forming black-shirted militia cast its lengthening shadow on a Parliament which was rapidly losing dignity. While Rome and Italy were slithering into economic penury and social distress, the bickering went on at Montecitorio. One of the most painful experiences De Gasperi had to endure was to see the former Socialist, Mussolini, once sent to fight De Gasperi in the Trentino, now able to exploit the parliamentary performance of democratic parties which were bordering on the disgraceful. Mussolini was able to rally support for his anti-parliamentary theories from some so-called democratic parliamentarians who, losing confidence in parliamentary procedures, were searching for a saviour for a nation threatened by political chaos of their own making. This chaos was being skilfully exploited also by the equally dictatorial anti-parliamentarians, the Communists, who were making their influence felt in the growing vacuum created by democratic party strife.

De Gasperi noticed dangerous erosion setting in even amongst the ranks of his own Popolari. When the King approached the Popolari deputy Filippo Meda, asking him to form a government, after a number of other coalition governments had failed, Meda did not even consult his party. Confronted with this responsibility, he seemed incapable of facing it and simply left Rome, refusing the King's commission. Don Sturzo was beside himself at this flight from responsibility of one of his senior political students. The result was that the King turned to Luigi Facta, a member of the long discredited party of Giovanni Giolitti, Prime Minister of many succeeding and unsuccessful governments. Facta failed to receive support either from Vittorio Emanuele Orlando on the right or from Enrico De Nicola on the left, and also had to give up in failure. As Andreotti wrote[1] "The sterility of the Socialists, the indecisiveness of the Catholics, the tolerance amounting to consent of the Liberals made Mussolini rapidly understand that it would be child's play to assume the role of the conqueror. Thus came the march on Rome and a new coalition government, presided over by Mussolini, in which he was able to include a number of representatives of the left and right as well as of the Popolari."

[1] Ibid., page 146.

Co-operation with members of the Popolari was arranged by Stefano Cavazzoni, who had maintained personal relations with Mussolini, his fellow Lombard, in the days of Mussolini's political activities as a Socialist in Milan. Their relationship had been maintained despite De Gasperi's opposition. De Gasperi's position as leader of the parliamentary party permitted him to make public admonitions to his party members who had accepted service under Mussolini. He urged them at least to respect in their new post the principles the party had maintained in the economic and social field, and in a speech in Parliament made a strong appeal for the preservation of liberty and legality. It was this speech which annoyed Mussolini who correctly read into it a criticism of his Fascist aims. At a party congress shortly thereafter, De Gasperi's speech was echoed by the acknowledged head of the party, Don Sturzo, in which he gave an outline of political aims for the party which Mussolini described as "that of an enemy". With the rising belligerency of the Fascists, Don Sturzo considered it wise to resign as political secretary of the party, "in order not to involve, as a priest, the Church in conflict with the Government". That was on July 10th, 1923. The same day debate began in Parliament on a bill introduced by the Fascist Minister of Agriculture, Acerbo, which became known as the *Legge Acerbo*. This bill provided Mussolini with the necessary powers to establish his dictatorship, should his party have a plurality of votes in the next elections, which would automatically allow them to obtain the majority of seats in the House. This would then enable the Fascists to vote absolute power to Mussolini, thus changing the basic principles of Italian parliamentary government.

The worsening economic situation, Italy's international political impotence because of her inability to establish a strong government, a rising wave of nationalism born of growing resentment at the treatment Italy had received at the hands of her war-time allies at the Versailles Peace Conference, were all cleverly exploited by Mussolini to assure himself a parliamentary majority. An interview between De Gasperi and Mussolini, in which De Gasperi tried to induce Mussolini to modify his new electoral law, led nowhere. Mussolini knew he need make no concessions to De Gasperi, because De Gasperi's own party was being adroitly disintegrated by Fascist blandishments to individual members. The Liberals early on threw their support behind Mussolini's law. Giolitti and his Liberal followers assured tolerance under the slogan "Possibilismo". The parties of the centre with their spokesman Giorgio Amendola and Ivanoe Bonomi, assured support because they did not want to create another governmental crisis. The Popolari were split, and when the vote came, De Gasperi found himself amongst 39 party members out of a total of 107 Popolari who voted against the *Legge Acerbo*. In the final vote Mussolini obtained a majority of 21 and, therefore, if he obtained a plurality in an election, a contingency which was more than likely, a dictatorship for Italy was assured.

This was the beginning of the end. Like Adolf Hitler, years later, when he split the German Catholic party, the *Zentrum*, and obtained a parliamentary majority for his "Empowering Laws", which eventually led to the abolition of parliamentary democracy, Mussolini had obtained, by democratic vote and parliamentary process, the abolition of parliamentary democracy. The German and Italian experiences of how negatively democracy can exercise its vote and accede to its own destruction, should be remembered by those who see in counting noses the be-all and end-all of true liberty.

When demagogy can incite emotions a majority vote can become a danger to liberty. Only when people's rights can be safeguarded constitutionally beyond the reach of treacherous mass reactions, rights to be embedded in law and safeguarded by an incorruptible judiciary, can parliamentary democracy be preserved against the predatory potential of majority votes.

Thus on July 15th, 1923, only two years after De Gasperi had been elected to the Italian Parliament, the Italian Parliamentary Government voted to abolish itself. De Gasperi's earlier battles against injustice in the Austrian Parliament were now to take on an even more sinister aspect in the Italian government under Benito Mussolini.

An interesting corollary to a parliamentary government voting themselves out of power under a constitutional monarchy and thus in a way also disenfranchising a constitutional monarch was given by King Victor Emanuel. On the twenty-fifth Anniversary of the King's accession to the throne, a number of opposition papers like the *Corriere della Sera* of Milan, *La Stampa* of Turin and the *Giornale d'Italia* of Rome, together with twenty-five provincial dailies, published an address of homage to the king, in which they reminded him of the occasion twenty-five years earlier when he had taken an oath to uphold the Constitution. The papers publishing this address were sequestrated by Mussolini. But through his Adjutant General, Arturo Cittadini, the king managed to let it be known that this reminder had been relayed to the "President of the Council of Ministers" (Mussolini). When, a little later, the king granted an audience to parliamentary opposition leaders, namely to Amendola, Di Cesaro and De Gasperi in order to hear their report on the constitutional situation, they again brought up the question of the constitutional obligations of the monarch, and he listened to them attentively but indicated that constitutional elections to a constitutional parliament, with a constitutional majority voting on a law, leave no legal leeway for a constitutional monarch. It will be recalled that years later, when the constitutionally established Grand Council of the Fascist party voted against Mussolini, the king ordered his arrest. While it might be claimed that this incident revealed a rather rigid line of constitutional thinking on the part of the king, it also throws an interesting light on the fallacy of the theory of parliamentary infallibility in the exercise of its suffrage. Certainly Hitler's dictatorship as well as Mussolini's, unlike the Communist dictatorship in Russia and later dictatorships in other Communist countries, had a legal parliamentary majority to fall back upon in its claims that it was legitimately elected as the democratic administrators of the popular will, even whilst it was perpetrating its crimes.

It was a matter of months after Mussolini received his parliamentary approval of the *Legge Acerbo* that De Gasperi found himself a fugitive from Fascist injustice. But before taking direct action against him, Benito Mussolini apparently wished to settle some scores in revenge for the bitter polemics he had had in De Gasperi's hometown in the Trentino in 1909. Now Mussolini again crossed swords with De Gasperi, but only in a much stronger position. No longer an obscure Socialist agitator sent in from Milan, but the head of a Fascist government in Rome, he attacked De Gasperi in the meanest of all political polemics, namely as a man of questionable Italian loyalty because he had been an Austrian citizen. He had him called an *Austriacante*, an Austrian fellow-traveller. Not only did the Fascist papers try to play on De Gasperi's "foreign birth", but they even produced a series of fake documents in order to throw doubts on his loyalty to the Italian cause in those days. In 1922 Mussolini had launched an attack on De Gasperi in his Fascist paper in Milan, *Popolo d'Italia*, of which he was editor, but he found himself rebuked by another Fascist newspaper, the *Era Nuova* of Trieste. The Trieste Fascist newspaper was constrained to publish a defence of the man who had done so much for the Trieste Italian population when Italians were bitterly persecuted by the Austrian authorities during World War I. But things were different in 1924 when Mussolini had established his dictatorship. Now the neswpapers in Italy were muzzled and it was a one-sided polemic, the only rebuttals voiced by newspapers abroad, whose voices no longer penetrated the Fascist censorship in Italy.

The personal denigration of De Gasperi launched by Mussolini was soon abandoned for more direct action; the arrest and even murder of political opponents was considered more effective. As terror spread in Rome, De Gasperi had taken refuge in the North amongst his mountaineer friends at Valsugana, while many of his other collaborators sought safety by fleeing abroad. De Gasperi had hoped to meet the opposition member of Parliament, Amendola, who had left for the North to take a cure at the spa of Montecatini. At the last minute De Gasperi received some private information that Mussolini's *Squadristi* (Stormtroopers) were on the rampage in that area and that Amendola was in danger. He wrote Amendola not to come, but unfortunately his letter arrived too late. Amendola was arrested, severely beaten and died as a result of his injuries.

Shortly thereafter two plainclothes men arrived at Valsugana to prepare for an unobtrusive arrest of De Gasperi, who was well known and liked by the villagers. On November 6th, in the middle of the night, he and his brother Augusto were arrested and the two were abducted secretly for fear of popular reaction. They were brought to Vicenza for questioning. A dangerous interrogation by the local police at Vicenza was fortunately cut short by the unexpected arrival of the Fascist member of Parliament for that district, Gaetano Marzotto, of the well-known industrial family. Marzotto had heard of the arrest of De Gasperi and feared that the worst might befall. Using his authority as a member of Parliament and of the Fascist party, Marzotto took the prisoner for "special investigation" under his personal charge. The fact was that he brought the two brothers to his country home at nearby Valdagno, gave them a chance to rest after their terrifying experiences at the hands of police investigators, and the next day took them to Verona in his own car and put them on the train for Milan. In Milan De Gasperi was able to hide for two months, and there news reached him that the 124 deputies who had left in protest against the murder of the Socialist Matteotti (the so-called Aventine-group of whom De Gasperi was one), had been declared expelled from Parliament and that consequently their parliamentary immunity had been lifted. In fact, this immunity was not too well respected by Mussolini's terror squads, but at least it had seemed to be some formal protection. Incidentally, the vote abolishing parliamentary immunity for the Aventine group, the so-called Turati Resolution, was passed unanimously by a Parliament which still included many members of the Liberal party, the Popolari and other groups, as well as the Fascists.

Immediately after the Turati Resolution was passed, new orders for De Gasperi's arrest were issued, and the hitherto evasions from arbitrary police violence now became flight from legalised police pursuit. Thus began a clandestine existence for De Gasperi, of changing residences and living under assumed names, which lasted for many months. But on March 11th, 1925 he was discovered near Orvieto on a train, accompanied by his wife, en route to his northern home from Rome.

This time the regime saw no need for a secret trial, as had happened in Vicenza. But as a precautionary measure to avoid warning his political friends, the Italian press received a circular telegram, instructing them to ignore the arrest of the well-known deputy. By keeping the arrest secret, the Government hoped to discover further evidence of conspiratorial action. They did not have to go far to seek evidence of De Gasperi's anti-Fascist sentiments, which he had himself quite openly expressed even in conversations with Mussolini. What they were also seeking was incriminating material for further arrests among De Gasperi's associates. They did find a list of addresses in De Gasperi's possession of many political associates. This alone was incriminating enough to subject them to special harassment and often even to arrest.

Under the charge of presumed flight abroad, of which no actual evidence existed, De Gasperi was condemned to prison. That the Italian Government did not take the charge seriously, was illustrated when they gave him leave to visit his dying father in Trent. He was condemned to four years in prison and a 20,000 lire fine was imposed on April 10th, 1927. On appeal, this was reduced to two years and a 16,000 lire fine, still tantamount to De Gasperi's complete destitution since it far exceeded his actual possessions.

Handcuffed, he was brought to the Regina Coeli prison in Rome. His health had been seriously affected both by the prison confinement previous to the trial and the treatment received after the judgment, when he developed serious gastric and kidney complications. These complications were not cured by his transfer as a prisoner to the Ciancarelli Hospital, but affected him for the rest of his life and were the cause of his premature death.

A year after De Gasperi's imprisonment, King Victor Emanuel visited Trent on the occasion of the inauguration of a monument to Cesare Battisti, the Socialist deputy in the Austrian Parliament whom the Austrians hanged on a charge of treason. It will be recalled that De Gasperi and Battisti were members of the same group of Trentino deputies, but now Battisti was being honoured as a champion of his people in the struggle on behalf of the Italian minorities, while the other champion was in prison. During the ceremony, the Archbishop of Trent, Celestino Endrici, who had himself been exiled by the Austrians, now resplendent in his full canonical robes for the occasion, unexpectedly turned to the King during the commemorative address, and said, "Sire, may we ask you for a favour which is close to everyone's heart here?" The King nodded assent. In a loud voice the Archbishop then said, "Liberate Alcide De Gasperi, unjustly condemned". The King gave an evasive answer, but shortly thereafter, in July 1928, a royal amnesty was issued, releasing De Gasperi from prison and permitting him to move to the Hotel Santa Chiara in Rome as a fixed, but supervised residence. His family was living at Valsugana, and later De Gasperi was joined occasionally by Signora Francesca, his wife, who divided her time between her children and visits to her husband, confined to forced residence in Rome.

But the problem facing De Gasperi was not only one of liberty. Having been completely impoverished by the fine, he had to earn a living not only for himself, but also for his family. According to his biographers, this was a time when he was sending what little money he could occasionally earn to his family, and himself frequently went hungry. There were times when he was unable to provide either for his family or for himself. Now and then he would get a little translation work, but he found that nobody wanted to give regular employment to this proclaimed "enemy of the state", for to do so would have been dangerous for the employer. Here and there De Gasperi picked up a few lire, giving lessons to children needing special tutoring for their exams. It was his early mentor and friend, Archbishop Endrici, who eventually obtained for him a desperately needed assignment to translate a book from the German. With that commission came an advance payment which permitted him to revive after a period of actual acute malnutrition which seriously affected his liver and left complications from which he suffered for years.

In those days of physical exhaustion, the humiliation of constant surveillance by secret police agents assigned to his hotel, who watched his every move day and night, of political despair and the spiritual trial of hopelessness, came the news of the final result of the accord between the Church and the Italian state—the Lateran Treaties. By these treaties, signed in 1929, the Church obtained the return of certain of her rights in education and in the maintenance of religious institutions taken from her at the time of the establishment of the Italian state in 1863.

De Gasperi's persecutors, the Fascists, obviously gained a political advantage. It is noteworthy that in three letters dated January 12th, 21st and 26th, 1929, while deeply conscious of this advantage, De Gasperi emphasised that as a Catholic, he must not be blind to the importance of the Treaties to the Church. They would facilitate the teaching and pastoral mission of the Church, so grievously hindered till then amongst her people.

In these letters De Gasperi recounts how the various anti-clerical elements in Italy and even abroad seemed pleased with the Concordat. Referring to former French Premier and Foreign Minister Artistide Briand as one of those congratulating Mussolini, he admits that there are many reasons for the Church's enemies to rejoice. He could understand the distress of not a few faithful Catholics, but he asked, "When Pius VII signed the Concordat with Bonaparte, the libertine general, blasphemer and product of the (French) Revolution, did not the loyal Catholics, who had suffered exile and worse, accept the authority of former priests and bishops, reinstated by this Concordat? When Leo XIII made peace with Bismarck (after the persecution of the Church in the *Kulturkampf*), did he not do it holding his protective hand over the heads of Windhorst (the political leader of the Catholic *Zentrum*) and the German bishops who had suffered so much? In both cases the pain caused to the Catholics is understandable, but who could doubt that the Holy See safeguards in an astonishing way the interests of the Church? . . . The making of the agreement, looked at in the Italy of today, may appear as a success for the Government. But regarded in the context of world history it is a liberation for the Church and a stroke of good fortune for the Italian nation". This was a remarkable example of how De Gasperi, despite his own persecution by the Fascist regime, was able to maintain a true perspective of political horizons. In actual fact, the conclusion of the Lateran Treaty, which permitted the Church a certain freedom of action and recognised exterritorial and diplomatic privileges to the Holy See as fully sovereign over at least some ten acres or more of territory, brought great advantages to the Church. Immune from interference by the Italian state, the Church was at least able freely to contact Catholics throughout the world, and deal directly under diplomatic immunity with all foreign governments. It also brought aid to De Gasperi of which he was not aware at the time.

He was shortly to obtain, together with a modest position in the Vatican library, quasi-diplomatic immunity as a civil servant of the newly recognised sovereignty, the Holy See. Cardinal Tisserant, the prefect of the Vatican library, wrote to Count della Torre, editor of the *Osservatore Romano*, "Dr. De Gasperi, who entered the service of the Vatican on April 1st, 1929, as a supernumerary assistant, has done an excellent job for us in a far too humble capacity, in preparing a catalogue of all Catholic publications. The perfect command of the German language and the vast culture of Dr. De Gasperi have made him an unusual collaborator, I may even say an excellent and most distinguished collaborator . . . Dr. De Gasperi had acquired much merit in serving the Church in the past, before coming to the library. It was in consideration of this that we have welcomed him amongst us, primarily to save him and his family".

Mussolini was highly displeased with the Vatican over De Gasperi's appointment, fearing that his old enemy would become the political adviser of Pius XI, and asked for "the courtesy" from the Holy See of dispensing with the services of De Gasperi and other "caporioni popolari". Monsignor Borgognoni-Duca was instructed by Pius XI to reply to Mussolini: "What you ask for as an act of courtesy on our part would in fact be an act of meanness and complete incomprehension of the paternal conduct of the Holy Father. As far as De Gasperi is concerned, the Holy Father neither regrets nor will regret having given to an honest man and the good father of a family that bread which you have taken away from him".

It was a comparatively menial assignment which was given to De Gasperi at the Vatican library and some criticism was voiced at the time that it was not really in keeping with the dignity of a man of his calibre. But to De Gasperi it gave the modest means to banish want from his family, at least as far as food and immediate necessities were concerned. It also provided an opportunity for writing and at least some degree of diplomatic immunity to his person, although even before that immunity existed, De Gasperi had been using his pen to break through the wall of silence which Mussolini had thrown up between the regime's opponents and the public. He had actually managed to write some articles, while under close police observation. An interesting comment was made by De Gasperi himself, which he quotes in the introduction to a collection of his articles, essays and comments written between the years 1928 and 1944, published under the title *I Cattolici Dell'Opposizione Al Governo* (*The Catholics in Opposition to the Government*, Laterza-Bari, 1954). He says that the reader "must well note the dates of each article, because one, on the German Catholic Party, the *Zentrum* and the one on Corporatism were written in 1928. They appeared at the high tide of Fascism under the pseudonym of "Jaspar" and were written in a hospital where the writer was under constant police surveillance". It was not until a year later that he received the Vatican library appointment.

This appointment had one unexpected but important side effect. De Gasperi was also asked to contribute a column of comments on international affairs for the authoritative and widely circulated bi-weekly *Illustrazione Vaticana*. He signed his column as "Spectator". Until 1938 he was thus able to clarify, rectify and direct much of the thinking not only in Italy but also in France, Germany and other countries where the publication was eagerly sought, because censorship made such reading scarce. In this way De Gasperi was able to relay much of his message combatting dictatorships and advocating the restoration of freedom.

By his writings, De Gasperi helped to maintain a clear vision of the true values on which to base serious studies. It can be safely assumed that the pungent comments and learned analyses of

"Spectator" were read by two other Catholic men, much concerned with the turn events were taking. One of them was Konrad Adenauer, already feeling the repressive arbitrariness of Adolf Hitler in Germany, and the other, Robert Schuman, who was deeply concerned with the political disintegration in his own country, with the obvious approach of France's hour of trial. Both shared De Gasperi's belief, both shared his scale of values in social and political matters. All three had been profoundly affected by the impact of Leo XIII's *Rerum Novarum.* They had many common interests, even if they had not yet met.

Since one of the big problems involved in the rise of the totalitarian regimes in Western Europe was the problem of applied democracy, and since the idea of democracy was largely attributed to political forces which had been released through the French Revolution, De Gasperi's studies and writings of those years concentrated attention in this direction. As a student of history, he was well aware of the alacrity with which the theoretically freedom-loving French, heirs to the French Revolution, accepted the dictatorship of Napoleon Bonaparte and, after a short revolutionary interregnum followed by a monarchial restoration, the actual dictatorship of Napoleon III. Had he lived long enough, he would have observed the same phenomenon in the years of acceptance by the French of de Gaulle's authoritarian one-man rule.

A convinced democrat, De Gasperi's strength also lay in the fact that he was a realist, and differed considerably from those apostles of democracy whose heads were in the clouds and whose feet were still bogged down in the eighteenth century of the Encyclopedists. De Gasperi knew only too well how such men, through their very lack of realism, had been willing, if blind, grave-diggers for their very principles by refusing to let parliamentary democracy have the necessary safeguards against extremist demagogues. Some of these "idealists" started by proclaiming greater liberties, only to end up as personal dictators. Mussolini, the Socialist, was a prime example. During the years De Gasperi spent under the Fascist regime, he not only observed and learned much for his future benefit, he never really ceased to fight for his ideas.

He was unable in those days to engage in political attacks against Mussolini's regime, even when writing under the pseudonym "Spectator", but he used his columns on foreign affairs in various publications and under various names to deal with Fascism's blood relation, Nazism. Since both Fascism and Nazism expounded the same principles, he was in fact attacking both. Thus in October, 1938 he devoted his column in the last issue of *Illustrazione Vaticana* before publication ceased, to a speech made by Joseph Kennedy, then Ambassador of the United States in London,[1] in which he drew a clear distinction between the rights of Caesar and the rights of God, and dealt with matters of religious liberty. De Gasperi added his own defence of the rights of confessional schools in Austria, then under attack by the Nazis, and devoted considerable space to the declaration of the German bishops on the occasion of the arrest by the Nazis of the Bishop of Rothenburg, Monsignor Sproll. "It was such a frankly courageous anti-Nazi declaration", De Gasperi commented on Monsignor Sproll's stand, "that it can only evoke the admiration of the entire world. It must be said that the serious events in Germany have also found men who can face them with dignity. Reading these apostolic words evoked a wave of admiration and pride and the people who heard them in the churches of Bavaria, the Rhineland, in Silesia and in the diaspora had, besides tears in their eyes, the presentiment of certain victory in their hearts". As the Church was suffering similar attacks in Italy, with violence to churchmen at the hands of the Fascists, the implications for domestic conditions were obvious.

A particularly delicate situation arose for De Gasperi when in 1940 Italy declared war on the side of Germany. Politically as well as militarily the deterioration of the Fascist regime became ever more evident, and the time soon came when De Gasperi found it necessary to prepare for the day when he could again take an active part in the political and national rehabilitation of Italy. This meant making more direct contacts with political leaders of other groups, in order to plan and prepare. So as not to embarass the Vatican by his direct political involvement, which now seemed necessary, De Gasperi abandoned the comparative security, economic and political, of the life of a Vatican civil servant. He went "underground" until the time of Mussolini's fall.

Hence we may say that Alcide De Gasperi actually commenced his political activities even before Mussolini was ousted, when the outcome of the war seemed to him certain and the need to prepare for post-war reconstruction imperative. He multiplied his political activities on two fronts. His first and principal aim was to establish some sort of team to replace his former party. In the twenty years of Fascist police persecution the *Popolari* had practically ceased to exist. This was in no small measure because of its own disintegration at the time of Mussolini's first coalition government, when a number of his own party had voted for the so-called *Legge Acerbo* which gave Mussolini extraordinary powers and thus legalised the establishment of his dictatorship. Nor must it be forgotten that in those twenty

[1] Father of assassinated President John F. Kennedy and Senator Robert Kennedy.

years many men had died and others had emigrated to distant lands, as political refugees. But there were some, comparatively few, former associates of De Gasperi with whom he could take up contact and who had rallied round him, such as Giovanni Gronchi, for example. Thus De Gasperi began recruiting a number of young men, mostly from among members of Catholic Action movements. From this group he recruited Giulio Andreotti, who was later to become a Cabinet Minister and who wrote, "We young men could not give as our contribution anything else but a passionate desire to heal with the balsam of political doctrine, inspired by Christian teachings, the deep wounds inflicted upon our nation, which was battling against all types of personal vengeance, defamation upon defamation and violence upon violence".[1]

But to rally men around him for the day when political activity would be possible did not satisfy De Gasperi. Once he had recruited cadres, he immediately set them to work, not in clandestine terror activities, but study. He divided them into study groups to train them for future roles in government. During the entire period of German occupation, for example, he set his newly organised followers to study the Social Code of Malines and documents on the Church's social teachings. At the home of Sergio Paronetto, De Gasperi arranged three weekly seminars at which prominent political and economic experts such as Professor Vannoni, the Spanish Jesuit Ulpiano Lopez, and Professor Pasquale Saraceno would give seminars on contemporary problems which any new government in a free world would face. Such groups were established also in Milan, which De Gasperi secretly visited in 1942, as well as in other centres. It must not be overlooked that although he did not participate in clandestine violence and terror, his activities and particularly his trips exposed him to exactly the same dangers, should he have fallen again into the hands of Mussolini's police, and therefore required great determination and even greater courage.

De Gasperi took refuge in the Seminary of St. John Lateran which, as an exterritorial area of the Vatican, had become a sanctuary for political refugees to whom the Vatican, as a sovereign state, granted this internationally recognised privilege. As a political refugee De Gasperi could now share his dangers with other political refugees and establish contacts, and here a very important and interesting aspect of De Gasperi's new political involvement must be noted. He had opposed the Austrian regime in the Trentino and he opposed Fascism in Italy, but always as a politician and champion of ideas, never engaging in conspiratorial, direct terrorist action against

[1] *De Gasperi e il Suo Tempo*, Giulio Andreotti (Mondadori, Milan, 1956).

constituted authority, whether in the Austro-Hungarian Empire or the Fascist regime he abhorred. In this he shared a common trait with Konrad Adenauer and Robert Schuman; none of them was involved at any time in the terrorist underground. They always regarded political terror acts with suspicion, both as to their effectiveness as well as a contradiction in principle to the restoration and the safeguarding of freedom, law and justice.

De Gasperi was certain that Fascism would crumble. But he was equally certain that the Italian soldiers, sailors and airmen were fulfilling their legitimate duty in an unfortunate war, a war in which they could demand patriotic loyalty from their co-citizens, for whom they were asked to offer their lives. There was no unity on this point amongst the anti-Fascist leaders in sanctuary at St. John Lateran. Some of them saw in sabotage and direct action, even at the cost of sacrifice of their own countrymen in the armed forces, a speeding-up of the defeat of Mussolini. De Gasperi, on the other hand, felt that no new society could be built on chaos. He feared that this would later undermine civic duty and the responsibility of the citizen towards the state, which could only lead to anarchy. De Gasperi considered that his Communist fellow refugees were as anxious to destroy a Fascist Italy as they were opposed to a democratic Italy, as both merely impeded the establishment of a Moscow-directed satellite totalitarian dictatorship. To De Gasperi the political battle of the future among the Italian parties, had to await the cessation of hostilities against foreign enemies. In the meantime, as Giulio Andreotti wrote in his book on De Gasperi,[1] the honour of the Italian flag had to be respected.

It was a very mixed group of men who were hidden at St. John Lateran. There were Jews shielded by the Vatican against the cruel anti-semitic depredations; there were political refugees such as De Gasperi, Ivanoe Bonomi the Liberal, Pietro Nenni the left-wing Socialist, and Giuseppe Saragat the moderate Socialist. There were military men who had too openly declared their disapproval of Mussolini, like General Bencivenga. The situation became particularly serious for all of them after German troops took control of Rome.

Like the others in the Seminary, De Gasperi was living in a room which was registered under the name of an absent seminarian, whose name the refugee took as a cover during his residence there. Thus De Gasperi became Alfonso Porta, later a parish priest in Rome. The refugees were under the particular care of Monsignor Ronca and Father Palaccini, who became experts both at camouflaging the

[1] *De Gasperi e il Suo Tempo* (Mondadori, Milan, 1956), page 186.

comings and goings of refugees and arranging for clandestine encounters with members of their families in dark corners of the cathedral of St. John Lateran. Signora Francesca, De Gasperi's wife and his daughter Maria Romana, were frequent visitors.

The question of feeding the refugees, whose number at times exceeded 800, was ably handled by priests. With praiseworthy ingenuity they had also granted refuge to a number of pure-bred cows, brought in from a nearby farm to save them from being "sequestrated" by German troops. Within the compound of St. John Lateran, these cows ensured a much-needed supply of fresh milk in critical times.

On Sundays Monsignor Alberto Ferrero de Cavallerleone, an army chaplain, later to become Archbishop and Chief Chaplain of the Order of Malta, came to say Mass, with De Gasperi active as the server. The camaraderie between the devout De Gasperi and non-believing friends like Nenni and others, is well illustrated by the teasing De Gasperi often received; they wondered whether he had not really missed his vocation as sacristan. The one thing that grew up amongst men of such varied convictions, religious as well as political, was respect for each other through their common bond of danger and opposition to the regime in power. Andreotti recalled how one Sunday, when Nenni had his radio on too loudly during Mass, another non-believer, the Liberal Bonomi, reprimanded Nenni, who carefully observed the necessary silence on following occasions. When things got too dangerous, De Gasperi moved to another refuge, the Propaganda Fide Palace, off the Piazza di Spagna, also a building enjoying exterritorial privileges as a possession of the Vatican.

* * *

Konrad Adenauer's tribulations started later than De Gasperi's but were no less dramatic. He had assumed his new and responsible duties as Lord Mayor of Cologne, as political life gradually emerged from the immediate post-war crisis.

Widowed in 1916 Konrad Adenauer married Gussi Sinser, who was eighteen years his junior, in September 1919. Both Gussi and her mother had been very kind neighbours after the death of Emma Adenauer, looking after the orphaned children, having them play in their garden and keeping an eye on them while Adenauer himself was deeply involved in his mayoral responsibilities. The Sinser and Adenauer gardens abutted and the children had grown very fond of their eighteen year old playmate, who three years later was to become their step-mother. Canon Hans Adenauer, attached to the Cologne Cathedral and brother of Konrad, married the couple. The marriage was to last happily for a quarter of a century, ending with Gussi's premature death from lasting injuries suffered during her incarceration by the Nazis.

By 1926 Konrad Adenauer had become a leading personality in Germany, not only as a powerful leader in the Catholic Centre Party Council, but also as an authoritative voice on questions of economic and cultural development. As the political situation of the Weimar Republic deteriorated due to party political strife in the Reichstag, his name was being mentioned frequently as a possible saviour, as Chancellor of a Grand Coalition, since he enjoyed the respect, if not necessarily the affection, of the Social Democrats as well as of the middle parties and conservative groups. He was actually summoned to Berlin in 1926 and offered the chancellorship, but after studying the situation with party leaders, he found it impossible to bring them together and returned to Cologne.

There have been speculations as to whether Adenauer could have stemmed the tide of disintegration of the Reich's parliamentary structure, which eventually culminated in Hitler's taking power. Evidence seems to be overwhelming that the old classical adage, those whom the gods would destroy they first make mad, applied to the Weimar party politicians. There were almost two dozen parties in the Reichstag at that time. They tried to make a constitution work which was utterly unsuited to the heterogeneous groups of the German people with their many different traditions and differing historical backgrounds. It was an attempt to seek unity without diversity and to stretch over the procrustean bed of a centralised government one "German people", when in fact each component part had been formed by a divergent history and was proud of its separate tradition.

Churchill summed up this feeling in his communication to the military command when monarchies were abolished in 1918, the Kaiser, Kings and Dukes abdicating. Commenting on the abolition of German traditions and substitution of a centralised government, we find Churchill quoted by Golo Mann: "To the extent that the revolution (1918) hit the Kaiser and the princes, and almost no one but them, it hit a phantom. The princes had not caused the war and they had certainly not led it; after 1866 they had no power. They were innocent; the guilty—if it is possible to attribute guilt to a particular class of human beings—were very different people: the industrialists, the members of the farmer's federation, of the war aims movement, the hack writers and politicians. They had no qualms about throwing the princes overboard, harmless ballast which they did not care about, provided more important things remained safely stored in the hold of the ship. People believed that something had been achieved just by the establishment of the 'Republic', as though they were still living in the middle of the nineteenth century, when the fall of the monarchy might in fact have had creative significance. 'The German Reich is a Republic', said the first sentence in the new constitution. Unfortunately, this did not signify much".[1]

By 1933, Adenauer's stature had established him as a staunch opponent of Adolf Hitler, whom he often privately described as the "brown-shirted Bolshevik". On January 30th, the "Bolshevik" was entrusted by Paul von Hindenburg with the Reich's chancellorship. Heinrich Brüning, of the Centre Party to which Adenauer belonged, had refused his urgent plea during the previous year to tackle the deepening German economic crisis more imaginatively. Brüning steadfastly refused to inaugurate any special economic measures, making the stability of the currency his cardinal objective. "Brüning will hold on to the currency and drop the political reins of the Government from his hands. There is nothing left to stem the on-rush of disaster", Adenauer is quoted as saying after returning from his last visit to Brüning in Berlin.[2]

Trouble for Adenauer began practically the day the Nazis came to power. As Lord Mayor of Cologne, he refused to hoist the Nazi flag, which was to him merely a symbol of a political party. He saw no reason why a party flag should be placed over the buildings of his ancient city, particularly to celebrate a Nazi chancellor. As Lord Mayor he insisted he had to be neutral and above any party preferences.

A fortnight after becoming Chancellor, Hitler came to Cologne to address a National Socialist Party rally for the forthcoming election. Adenauer considered the occasion merely the electioneering visit of a party chief and refused to extend an official welcome to the new Chancellor. A few days later he had the swastika flags struck from a Rhine bridge, where enthusiastic Storm-troopers had hoisted them, because it was municipal property. With angry Storm-troopers looking on, Cologne police took down the flags on the Chief Magistrate's direct orders.

On election day, March 12th, Konrad Adenauer attended a memorial service for the war dead. It was his last appearance in public in Cologne for twelve years. That afternoon he received a warning that the Storm-troopers (SA) had been ordered to liquidate him in his office the next day. He sent his wife to the Catholic Caritas Hospital at Hohenlinde, where his children had been sent

[1] *The History of Germany Since 1789*, Golo Mann (Chatto & Windus, London; Frederick Praeger, New York), page 337.
[2] *Konrad Adenauer*, Paul Weymar (André Deutsch, London), page 97.

earlier as a precautionary measure against possible SA attacks on his home. He waited till dark, and then left by car for Dortmund where, unobserved, he caught the train for Berlin in order to lodge a complaint, against illegal interferences, with the Prussian Minister of Interior in Hitler's new Government, namely with Herman Goering himself. As Adenauer arrived in Berlin, the Cologne papers were headlining, "Dismissal of the Lord Mayor for desertion from his post". Simultaneously the local provincial government authorities issued a formal order, prohibiting the entry of the Lord Mayor into Cologne or its government district. He was in fact exiled.

Still Adenauer would not bend. His ousting from the presidency of the Prussian Upper House was to follow apace, but this could only be achieved by the Upper House in session. The Socialist Prime Minister of Prussia, Dr. Otto Braun, had fled to Switzerland. Franz von Papen, the newly appointed Reichskommissar for Prussia, took it upon himself to summon the Upper House of Prussia to a session, in order to dissolve it and thereby terminate Adenauer's office. Adenauer, as President, denied von Papen the legal right to act and refused to sign the decree. This was defiance by a man who no longer had anything to aid him except his character and his convictions. He knew as well as anyone else that he could not hold back the tide of power of the Nazis. The Nazi Government ratified von Papen's summons and dissolution, and thus lifted the immunity of the President of the Upper House. All that Adenauer wanted to achieve, and had achieved, was to underline the illegality of the Prussian action. But the Nazis were furious at what they considered had been an affront and a public defiance, and Adenauer's bank account was sequestrated. All payments due him as Lord Mayor and a member of the Upper House were blocked, pending a trumped-up charge of corruption brought against him as Mayor. Actually, the Nazis had to drop the charge but were not slow to invent another, which proved as groundless. Meantime these charges served the purpose of rendering Adenauer completely destitute.

Help came from a most unexpected quarter, and arrived when it was most needed. Many of Adenauer's political and professional associates were shunning the man who was so obviously on the Nazi's proscribed list, but at that moment a wealthy German-American friend, Mr. D. N. Heinemann, who lived in Brussels, decided to come to Berlin. He looked up Adenauer and handed him 10,000 marks in cash, ". . . . because you might have difficulties cashing a cheque". Adenauer at first protested against such lavish aid and refused to accept it, stating that his salary had been blocked, his property "frozen", and that as he saw no visible means of repayment, he had no right to borrow the money. Heinemann found in these excuses the justification of his action, telling Adenauer that he wanted neither receipt, I.O.U. nor promise of repayment and that, incidentally, he was extremely busy. Taking his leave he disappeared as hurriedly as he had come. Adenauer was left nonplussed and deeply moved. When he made his first official visit to the United States in 1953, his first call was on his friend Heinemann in New York.

As Adenauer knew that his arrest by the Berlin Gestapo was imminent, he slipped away to the world famous Benedictine Abbey of Maria-Lach, where his former classmate Ildefonso Herweegen was Abbot and had offered him sanctuary. Adenauer remained there undiscovered for almost a year. He devoted a great deal of time to re-reading and studying the two great Papal encyclicals *Rerum Novarum* and *Quadragesimo Anno*, making elaborate notes. It was from these two encyclicals, Adenauer would often say, he received the urgent warning against expanding the power of the state at the expense of the personal liberties of every individual. These documents had similarly served as texts for careful study to Alcide De Gasperi and to Robert Schuman.

Separation from the family was the most painful of his many sufferings during exile and hiding, and it was of particular comfort to receive a visit during the summer from Paul, the ten year old son of his second marriage. Father and son attended the choir services of the monks and went for long walks in the adjoining woods. The boy later became a priest, Father Paul Adenauer, and frequently recalled the deep impression his father's profound faith and their many talks had made on him during that visit to Maria-Lach.

The desire for a reunion with his family led to an imprudent move. When Christmas came, there was a happy family gathering in the nearby hotel, where rooms had been taken. The hotel lay isolated in the Eifel mountains, deep in winter snow, and was therefore considered safe. Gussi Adenauer with her four children and the three children from the first marriage all arrived for the occasion. Soon, however, the Nazi authorities picked up the scent they had lost and discovered Adenauer's whereabouts. The Abbot received peremptory orders from the provincial governor not to grant further sanctuary to this "enemy of the state". Although the Abbot angrily rejected the demand, Adenauer felt that he could no longer expose the Abbot and monks to reprisals. As there had never been a warrant issued for his arrest, he took the chance of losing himself again in the capital and went to Berlin.

A house in the suburb of Neu-Babelsberg was put at his disposal by people who had decided to leave Germany. There the family was reunited and lived fairly unmolested for the next few months. The children often recalled in later years the many happy moments they had spent with their father, a unique experience dividing the previous bitter years from those to come. As all his money was blocked he could only dispose freely of the collection of paintings he had accumulated through the years for his own pleasure as an amateur art collector. Now the family lived from the sale of a good part of these paintings, unwilling to cut too deeply into the loan he had received from his friend Heinemann.

But the Nazis were not content to leave Adenauer alone for too long. Suddenly a summons was served on him to appear as a witness in an embezzlement charge levelled at a bank manager in Cologne. He was given special permission to go to Cologne. The bank manager was to be examined privately so as not to give Adenauer an opportunity of appearing in open court in public, and it was arranged that the meeting should take place at the home of Adenauer's brother, Canon Adenauer, in the parish residence on Cathedral Square. When the judge, prosecutor, accused, the court clerks and Adenauer were gathered to hear the charges of embezzlement against the bank manager, the accused suddenly turned to the gathering and stated, "The Lord Mayor is guilty of "passive bribery", having received 35,000 marks from the Deutsche Bank because of preferment shown to the bank by the Lord Mayor". Such an accusation before all the legal witnesses, unless it could be refuted then and there, would have involved a criminal indictment with the possibility of a criminal sentence of hard labour, whose real purpose would have been to exclude Adenauer forever from any political or public office, even after the Nazis had been ousted.

It was obvious to Adenauer that he was facing a dangerous frame-up and that the charges of embezzlement against the bank manager were being used by the Nazis to encourage the bank manager to extricate himself by levelling charges at the Lord Mayor. For hours a tense duel lasted between the untrustworthy bank manager and Adenauer, fighting both for his reputation as well as for his political future. He submitted the bank manager to gruelling cross-examination, entangled him in contradiction, disproved detail after detail in the charge, but still at fixed intervals the statement that the Lord Mayor had accepted a bribe was repeated. Every time the charge was made the court clerk took it down assiduously. This went on from early morning till late in the afternoon. Finally Adenauer, pointing to a crucifix on the wall, suddenly turned to his accuser and adjured him, "In the name of all that is sacred to you—tell the truth!" The witness broke down, admitting the frame-up, and was immediately savagely attacked by the prosecutor who thereby gave the whole show away. But even in the face of threats of dire punishment from the prosecutor there came the firm avowal, "My original statement was untrue. I withdraw my charge". This was the second trial for subversion of funds while in office the Nazis had framed up, and once again it had failed. This was in March 1934. Adenauer returned to his home in Neu-Babelsberg.

The date of June 30th, 1934 has gone down in history as the famous blood-purge of the so-called "Roehm revolt". At that time Hitler not only destroyed some of his friends who had brought him to power, but also a large number of political rivals like General Kurt von Schleicher and other people who had been generally inconvenient to him. On his particular list for the purge were some leading Catholics, men like Erich Klausner and others who lost their lives.

On the evening of that day a small car drove up to Adenauer's residence at Neu-Babelsberg and a member of the secret police ordered him to pack his bags and come along. The whole family stood around in consternation. The only one who seemed unperturbed was Adenauer himself, as he waved from the garden gate before getting into the police car.

Three frightening days followed. Adenauer was threatened with execution and torture unless he "confessed". The cross-examination lasted for hours. Then he was suddenly released. Orders had come from Hitler to stop all proceedings as his blood-lust had apparently been satiated by hundreds of murders of the most gruesome variety, and all prisoners still under examination were to be freed immediately. But that did not mean that the harassment and persecution of Adenauer ceased. He received a warning through his friend, the Abbot of Maria-Lach, that his assassination had been decided upon and was imminent. It was decided to leave Berlin, where an assassin could succeed more easily than in a small village. So the family moved to the obscure little village in the mountains of the Siebengebirge, not far from Cologne but outside its governmental district, called Roehndorf. The Nazis reacted by withdrawing permission for Adenauer to live also in that specific governmental district. Again he had to leave the family and move away.

Threats of arrest and continued chicanery became the rule, as the Gestapo agents would visit him at regular intervals wherever he had stopped. Friends recalled how after a few years of this hounded existence he suffered moments of complete despair. But he always managed to overcome his despondency, constantly seeking ways and means of surviving Nazi terror which he knew would have to come to an end some day.

There was a slight easing of the situation in 1936 when a new Lord Mayor succeeded the rabid Nazi, Günther Riesen, and let it be known through Adenauer's lawyer-brother, Dr. August Adenauer, that he felt the former mayor had been too harshly treated. A small compensation was paid for the two houses belonging to Adenauer which had been sequestrated, and part of his pension was released. With that money, and with the lifting of the ban to live in Roehndorf, Adenauer decided to purchase a piece of property in that village. It was an idyllic spot which became his home, and remained his residence even after he became Chancellor. The house in a beautiful garden, on the Zennigsweg, stood on a hill slope giving an unrestricted view of the Rhine valley, across to the Eifel mountains. For three succeeding years Hitler seemed to have forgotten his enemy, and the family led a comparatively quiet and undisturbed life. Only as some of the children married did any change occur. Then the war came. His sons, Max, Paul and finally Konrad were called to the colours. The daughters-in-law moved in and, except for his youngest son who was twelve years old, Adenauer found himself the only man in the house with eight women to care for.

It is interesting to note that during all that time Adenauer kept strictly away from any conspiratorial connections. His attitude to violence of a lawless nature was very much the same as that of Alcide De Gasperi. Both felt that one could not restore law and order by terror and coercion, and that legality and democracy could not be restored, firmly established and safeguarded by the use of illegality and force.

In 1943, he was approached by emissaries of the former Lord Mayor of Leipzig, Carl Goerdeler, to join an active opposition group, but Adenauer flatly refused. His aversion to violence seems only partly to have prompted his decision which was also influenced by the fact that he considered Goerdeler a rather fumbling politician. He feared that Goerdeler would be singularly inept in his plans and that any conspiracy of which he was the author would be doomed to failure, bringing in its wake new and even more violent repressions. Goerdeler was executed consequent to July 20th, 1944.

The events of July 20th included deeds of great heroism on the one hand and appalling blunders on the other, and unleashed a blood-bath of terrifying proportions, even for Hitler's reign of terror. Like a wounded beast, his thirst for revenge knew no bounds.

After the unsuccessful attempt by Count Stauffenberg on Hitler's life, there were three days of mass arrests not confined to those directly connected with the plot. The round-ups delivered to the terror of the courts and concentration camps not only Field Marshals, Generals and high officers but prominent members of the nobility, and others in the field of politics and religion. Father Delp and Dietrich Bonhoefer were among the victims. But the nobility in particular became the target of Hitler's fury. Wives, children and even distant cousins of those implicated in the plot were rounded up and turned over for "tribe-extermination". Men like Field Marshal von Witzleben were hanged alive on meat hooks, and beheading could rightly be considered mercy killing. To Adenauer and his family there were sufficient indications that Hitler would use this opportunity to eradicate and eliminate "once and for all" all his opponents, crush opposition and particularly any possible alternative to his rule. Adenauer's fears proved justified.

A few days later, while the family was at lunch, Gestapo agents arrived with a search warrant. For seven hours they ransacked every drawer, every book shelf and every file in the library, looking through all private correspondence. Then they affixed their lead seal to the door of Adenauer's study and left, but not for long. They were back the next day for further examinations. Then there was a fortnight's lull, to be followed by the inevitable and expected.

Early one morning in the middle of August, 1944, with Allied guns already audible in the distance, the Roehndorf policeman brought a Gestapo agent with a warrant for arrest. The poor local policeman, who knew Adenauer well, felt very badly about his mission and tried to convince Mrs. Adenauer and the family that they would see Konrad Adenauer back shortly. He was taken to the concentration camp improvised on the Cologne Exhibition grounds, where conditions of overcrowding, lack of sanitation and vermin were particularly bad.

For weeks, men from all walks of life and professions swelled the already too numerous ranks of earlier political prisoners. Nightly the ranks were thinned by special assignments of inmates sent to Büchenwald. These were never heard of again, except perhaps for a curt notification of their death to the family. While some reached Büchenwald and were executed there, most of them never arrived but were shot by their guards en route. The laconic communiqué, "Shot while attempting to flee", told the macabre story of summary execution on some dark road through the forest.

Adenauer was befriended by Eugen Zander, a once militant Communist, who had spent so many years in the camp that he was well known to the guards and was even given a small assignment by the prison authorities. At that time he was storekeeper, and noticed that the "Herr Oberbürgermeister" was really in a very bad physical shape, for Adenauer had become a wan shadow of himself, suffering both from malnutrition and insomnia. Actually Zander probably saved Adenauer's life. Not only did he give him a clean bunk in his own storeroom, where rest was easier than in the vermin-infested, unventilated barrack dormitory, but he also conspired to warn him and engineer his escape when things became critical.

One day Zander was cleaning the camp commandant's office in his usual routine, when he suddenly saw the time-table list for men to be transported to Büchenwald. He knew what it meant when he saw on the list for the day after tomorrow the name of Konrad Adenauer. He not only warned the Herr Oberbürgermeister of the danger, but set a special plan in motion. Adenauer was immediately put to bed with a heart-ailment and Doctor Richarz, a fellow prisoner assigned to medical duty in camp, was called. Let into the secret, he examined Adenauer and sent Zander for a prescription of symphatol from the dispensary. Spilling half the bottle instead of administering it, Doctor Richarz then called the camp commandant, informing him of Adenauer's cardiac crisis, demanding that he be removed immediately to the hospital in town, as he was likely to die. Frightened of losing any important prisoner through carelessness or inattention, the camp commandant had an ambulance called and Adenauer found himself a privileged patient in the Hohenlinde hospital in the care of his friend, Dr. Uhlenbruck, to whom he did not have to simulate. Actually, simulation had not been difficult to the near septuagenarian, emaciated prisoner who had survived torture, long hours of investigation, insomnia and constant anxiety. As his condition improved visibly, longer sojourn at the hospital became imprudent and another plot was concocted. Gussi Adenauer had been permitted to visit constantly at the hospital. One day an air-force major arrived with an imposing document bearing many seals, and demanded immediate custody of Dr. Adenauer, as he had to drive him to Berlin. The hospital authorities obeyed, and Adenauer found himself in an Air-Force car, his wife awaiting him in the back seat. The driver was his friend, Air-Force Major Hans Schliebusch. The drive finally ended, after a night's hideout in Bonn, way out in the country at Nister Muehle, an old water mill concealed in the Westerwald mountains near Koblenz. Gussi Adenauer went back to Roehndorf and in order to eradicate traces of the escape, went to the Gestapo and asked where her husband was, as he had suddenly disappeared. For a few weeks it looked as though the race against time between advancing Allied troops and Nazi terror would be won.

Then suddenly the Gestapo came and arrested Frau Gussi Adenauer. It was a traumatic experience for the poor woman, an emotional shock from which she never quite recovered. She was subjected to the most brutal interrogations for hours, by the dreaded Cologne Gestapo Commissar Bethge at the Brauweiler prison, and part of the frightening intimidation consisted in her being herded into a cellar room with a number of the town's prostitutes. To their hilarious jeering, she was introduced by a Gestapo guard as "a distinguished guest, Frau Oberbürgermeister". She cowered in a corner, while to the blare of a gramophone in the guard-room, these damsels lewdly swayed in frenzied dances to please their leering guards. After short intervals in these infernal sourroundings, Frau Adenauer would again be brought for an interrogation. Time and again she denied knowledge of her husband's whereabouts. When the grilling ended, she would be back in the cellar. Meantime the exhausted hussies had occupied every inch of space on the floor and were sleeping, and Frau Adenauer could only stand in the corner next to two tin buckets serving as toilets, the only furniture in the room, whose stench mingled with that of vile bodies and cheap perfume. Every few hours she would be led back for questioning, always to the one question fired at her, time after time: "Where is your husband?" Sometimes Bethge tried to cajole her and sometimes he would threaten. Then she would be led back again to the nightmarish cellar.

Finally, after a few days, Bethge played his most dastardly card. He suddenly shot a new question at the distraught and exhausted woman:

"How do you like your quarters?"

"It is hell", she replied.

He then informed her that whether or not she told him where her husband was they would be able to find Konrad Adenauer, and she would have to stay in prison until then.

"In the meantime, what about your daughters at home?" he asked. "What are their ages?"

"Nineteen and sixteen", Gussi Adenauer replied.

If she revealed the whereabouts of her husband, Bethge then told her, he could assure her that her husband would be treated more leniently than if he were found after a long search; she would be free to return home and nothing would happen to her daughters. If she refused, he would lock the girls up with the prostitutes, of whom enough were arrested every night to keep them company for as long as their father was not found.

"And how would you like that, Frau Adenauer?" he leered at her.

Terror stricken even at the thought of exposing her two girls to this obscenity, certain that her husband would never have forgiven her if he knew that his children were sacrificed in this way, she suddenly said, "He is in the Westerwald, at Niester Muehle".

Gussi Adenauer was sent back to the cellar while her information could be checked. That same night Adenauer was re-arrested and three hours after his incarceration he was brought before Commissar Bethge. With sadistic glee, Bethge told Adenauer that his wife had revealed his whereabouts, informing him at the same time with the pride of achievement how his threat regarding the daughters had worked. Konrad Adenauer, now a prisoner before him, gave a curt answer:

"She was right."

Then Bethge called for another prisoner to be brought up, in order to be released. It was Frau Gussi Adenauer. In passing, she saw her husband in the prison as she was about to leave.

Shortly after his recapture, Adenauer fell seriously ill and had to be transferred to a sick ward in the same prison. It was at Brauweiler prison, after his recovery, that orders were received for his release. Preparations were being made by the Nazis to shoot all the prisoners, should they have to evacuate because of the approach of U.S. troops, and in some cases the jailers were already pointing out the places near the wall where they would be shot. Konrad Adenauer's son, Lieutenant Max Adenauer, was contacted at the front in the hope that he might intervene, as the situation was precarious. He sped back from the Eastern Front only to hear of his father's capture, which had been kept secret until then, lest knowledge of Gestapo depredation should weaken the fighting spirit of the troops. Hoping to obtain his father's release, Lieutenant Adenauer went to the dread Gestapo headquarters at 10 Albrecht Strasse in Berlin, and as a result the Commissar received orders on Sunday night to release the prisoner. When Bethge told Adenauer that release papers had arrived and that he would release him on Monday, Adenauer insisted on his immediate release. Leaving his belongings in the prison's safe, which Bethge claimed was locked over the week-end, rather than spend another night at Brauweiler with the threat of instant execution hanging over all prisoners of war as the cannonade of advancing American troops became more and more audible, Adenauer left that same night. It was November 26th, 1944, right after a heavy air-raid on Cologne. About three months later, the Americans crossed the Rhine at the Remagen Bridge. In the middle of March, 1945, three American officers arrived at Roehndorf, asking Konrad Adenauer to accompany them immediately to Cologne where he was to assume the duties as civilian mayor of his native city of Cologne, which had been occupied by the U.S. troops.

But liberation did not restore everything in the Adenauer household. In the spring of 1947, the failing health of Gussi Adenauer, who had never recovered her former gaiety and energy after her dreadful prison experiences, began seriously to worry her husband. She had been suffering from deep depressions on and off since her release, and Adenauer devoted all his spare time from his political preoccupations to her. Finally she developed leukemia, as a direct after-effect of her physical trials and the torturing anxieties in the concentration camp, and in December of that year she had to be transferred to the hospital in Bonn. Her husband was able to summon world-famous specialists from Germany and Switzerland, but to no avail. She died on March 3rd, 1948. A month later, at the age of seventy-two, Konrad Adenauer was summoned to the State Parliament of North-Rhine-Westphalia, in the British Zone, to hear General Sir Brian Robertson announce the division of Germany into Western Germany and Soviet-occupied Eastern Germany. He heard the British General plead with the Germans to restore and reconstruct for themselves what the Allies had destroyed. Konrad Adenauer undertook that task.

* * *

As at the end of World War I De Gasperi faced the need to reorientate his interests and to study entirely different political, constitutional and juridical conditions necessitated by the integration of his homeland into Italy, so Robert Schuman faced the same situation when the hitherto Prussian provinces of Alsace-Lorraine again became French. They had been severed from the French kingdom under Napoleon III; they were reintegrated into a secularised Third Republic.

A Consultative Council at Strasbourg was established for Alsace-Lorraine to deal with the problems involved. Robert Schuman became its member for the Moselle area and later its President. It took some urging and very plain talk from his friends to persuade him to accept candidature in the first elections to the French Chamber for the *Union Républicaine Démocrate*. But once engaged in the political life of France, he developed a certain taste for defending his very determined views with opponents.

It was not long before he came into direct conflict with the "cartel of the Left" on questions of religious education and basic attitudes towards the state. The tone of his election speeches became yet more pronounced in the new elections in 1924, and in that year we read in the newspaper *L'Alsace Française* (December 13th) the following report of his speech on the question of education, which he made to his constituents after his successful election:

"Beware of those who want to put you to sleep . . . and want to introduce in stages, little by little, that which the very soul of the people of Lorraine rejected . . . They wish to stifle the life of religion in our land and in the people . . . For the love of your children, we want to prevent that happening".

In 1928, the proportional representation electoral system was replaced by the constituency system with run-off elections for a candidate who had not won an absolute majority. Schuman presented himself for the constituency of Thionville, his family's native area. He held the constituency by large majorities, being elected on the first ballot in the election of 1932 and again in 1936. It was largely a personal vote of confidence he received, since in 1931 he had left the *Union Républicaine* to join Raymond Laurent's *Parti Démocrate Populaire*, a very small party, but Schuman felt it gave wider scope to general problems, particularly in the search for a Franco-German understanding, which already interested Robert Schuman at that time. He found his former party, the *Union Républicaine Democrate*, somewhat too narrow and rigid on questions of foreign affairs, to which he was devoting more and more attention as the integration of Alsace-Lorraine proceeded apace.

Schuman was particularly sympathetic to the foreign policy initiated by Aristide Briand and his European Union and to the work of the League of Nations, and had a very clear concept of the issues at stake in the years between the two World Wars. He saw freedom and democratic regimes being eroded by greater authoritarianism in government which was leading to outright dictatorship as in Germany and Italy, or to varying degrees of authoritarian government, as in Poland and Lithuania, in Austria and Hungary, in Yugoslavia, Rumania, Spain and Portugal. He also observed this erosion leading to disintegration or political ineffectiveness, as in France under the Third Republic which foundered when war broke out in 1939 because of internal disruption. By that time, Parliamentary Democracy in its constitutional form was actually operative only in Great Britain, the Scandinavian countries, Holland, Belgium and Switzerland.

Democracy cannot be improvised, Robert Schuman maintained, pointing out that it took well over a thousand years for Christianity to develop in Europe. He often quoted Jacques Maritain and Bergson, when Maritain claimed that instincts and the power of the irrational are even stronger in the collective than in an individual Schuman felt that it was a confirmation of the view that the first step towards an orderly society is the discipline the individual citizen is willing to impose upon himself.

Summing up his views at the end of his life Schuman wrote: "democracy will either be Christian or it will not exist. An anti-Christian democracy will be a caricature which will founder into tyranny and anarchy."[1]

It was unthinkable to him that the state could systematically ignore the religious factor, taking an attitude bordering on the

[1] *Pour l'Europe*, Robert Schuman (Nagel, Paris).

hostile. Schuman felt that the state must realise the great role religious conviction plays in furthering civic virtues in a people. The Church should never play the role of policeman, but the great moral force represented by large numbers of religiously convinced citizens and the influence inherent in Christian teaching must never be under-estimated. The same applies, Schuman stressed, to the religious solidarity of the faithful of many countries, and to the beneficial influence which the Holy See exercised through its international independence, impartiality, and disinterestedness and universal charity.

The visits he made to various statesmen and political figures in other countries were not only a source of valuable information which widened his international horizons, but led also at times to dramatic revelations.

In 1932 he attended the Eucharistic Congress in Budapest. That year he also attended a Congress at Cologne, where Franco-German questions were discussed, but he did not meet Konrad Adenauer then.

The following year, after reading *La Yugoslavie en Péril* by his friend Ernest Pezet, he visited that country to see for himself. It was just before an official visit to France by King Alexander of Yugoslavia. Immediately upon his return on September 15th he wired his friend Pezet to meet him in Paris, as he had to speak to him urgently.

Schuman had met Croat leaders and had had a long audience with King Alexander. He confided what he had heard and what he had seen to his friend as they sat in a café on the Boulevard Raspail and together they composed an urgent message to the Quai d'Orsay, advising the Government to cancel the king's visit because of the very real danger of assassination by Croat terrorists.

Foreign minister Barthou read the message and passed word back that he considered the fears much exaggerated. Shortly after that the King arrived and he and Barthou were assassinated when the monarch was driven from his ship through the streets of Marseilles.

In 1938 Schuman visited Austria, studied the situation there under Hitler's rule, and met many people who had been in prominent positions, but whom the Nazis had ousted. This trip became the subject of lengthy interrogations by the Gestapo when Schuman found himself their prisoner after the collapse of France in 1940.

Schuman was particularly interested in political frontiers and once wrote that they were born of historical and ethnical evolutions which should be respected. No one should think of eradicating them. At certain times frontiers had been changed, either by violent conquest or by purposeful marriage contracts. But he saw in them the merit of gradually having given people a tradition and a solid internal structure. He also looked upon them, however, as solid foundations upon which new superstructures should be built. He was definitely opposed to the fusion of national States or the erection of super-States; what he sought was union, cohesion and co-ordination. Towards the end of his life, and looking back on it, he spoke of the harsh lessons history had taught a "borderland" man like himself, and one of these was to be suspicious of hurried improvisations and over-ambitious projects. But as a frontiersman he had also learned that when a decision has been reached by careful and mature reflection, soundly based on the reality of existing facts and clearly in the interest of the people, then there should be no hesitation in resolutely embarking on new and sometimes revolutionary enterprises, despite possible conflicts with established customs and deeply rooted prejudices.

As a man deeply involved in the policies of France, Schuman had some unpleasant experiences. One was the suspicion of some of the old French statesmen. Once he made representations to Georges Clemenceau on behalf of his Lorraine people: with icy disdain the "old tiger" blandly asked, "Who are the people from the Lorraine?" In 1926 there was another occasion when, as President of the Consultative Council, Schuman felt he had to make special representations to Raymond Poincaré in the interests of his people. Poincaré turned on Schuman with a harsh reproach, practically accusing him of placing the interests of his homeland above those of France, adding that this did not surprise him. This was very reminiscent of the attacks made upon De Gasperi by Italian politicians when the man from Trentino was inconvenient to them because of the principles for which he stood.

When war broke out in 1939, Schuman's first impulse was to return to his people in Metz and try, as a member of Parliament, to relieve their hardship. Then Paul Reynaud appointed him Under-Secretary for Refugees, and as the refugee problem primarily concerned the border folk from Alsace-Lorraine, Schuman felt that he could be more useful in that position. As the French state collapsed and the Government evacuated Paris he was often exposed to considerable personal danger as he worked incessantly to find food, lodging and medical care for the thousands who were fleeing from the Nazi troops. When the French Government finally collapsed and a new one under Field Marshal Pétain was established in Vichy, Schuman was offered a post in it but refused, returning instead to Metz to see what he could do for his people.

His freedom did not last long. He was arrested by the Gestapo and kept for months, first in prison under constant harsh cross-examination, and later in forced residence under police surveillance in a small town in Germany, whence he was deported. It was during these examinations that his visit to Cologne in 1932 was construed by the Nazis as an attempt at conspiratorial contact with Adenauer. First they tried to convince him that he could serve his people best by declaring himself sympathetic to the occupying German army. When this failed, they tried to terrorise him. Made aware of the danger of the concentration camp and all that it implied, he escaped. For weeks on end he wandered through the country under assumed names, using false papers made out in the name of Monsieur Cordonnier (the French for Schuman—cobbler), and at other times using his mother's maiden name of Duren, in an effort to reach the territory of the Vichy Government, where the Gestapo could not reach him. He hid in convents, he crossed forests on foot, he was aided by underground communications established by his friends and family and at last, in November 1943, he reached Bourg and was received at the orphanage of La Providence de Beaupont, his twelfth residence since he fled the Gestapo. There he remained until the liberation.

In the small room at the end of a corridor he received visits from some of his friends, including Senator René Jager. Jager recalls how, in those days, Schuman spent a great deal of time planning ways and means by which after hostilities had ceased a reconciliation between French and Germans could be effected, so that the tragedy he was then witnessing should never be repeated.

One day in August 1944 some of the children who had gone for a walk came back to the orphanage and said they had seen Americans. At first nobody would believe them, until they produced chewing gum, chocolate, canned milk, corned beef and other delicacies. The very next day Robert Schuman joined the citizens of Bourg to celebrate their liberation. In September 1944, General de Lattre de Tassigny needed a special adviser who was experienced in the politics of Alsace-Lorraine, and he sent one of his officers to find Schuman, who immediately began work under him. Three weeks later the Minister of War, Diethelm, noticed the name Robert Schuman listed as a government employee and immediately ordered the General to dismiss this "product of Vichy". De Lattre had no choice, but he asked Robert Schuman to take up his residence in the Moselle county and sent Henri Bayer, an officer of his General Staff and a friend of Schuman, to accompany him and afford protection against the petty persecutions so rife in France just then. The Americans lent him a jeep. The roads and bridges were severely damaged and the city of Metz still in German hands. They reached Evrange, near Metz, where he took up residence.

A few days later a summons was issued for Schuman's arrest as he was suspected of having collaborated with the Germans. His friends were shocked and scandalised that this man, the first French member of Parliament arrested by the Gestapo, who had throughout the war given ample proof of courage in defying the enemy and in helping his fellow countrymen, should be treated thus by the government of liberated France. On the advice of his friends Schuman disregarded the summons to go to Paris for questioning as he was warned that the wave of purges and terror unleashed by Communists and other groups, who had emerged from the underground to take personal and political revenge, had not yet subsided. When the moment was right, the Minister in charge of the Department of the Interior, Monsieur de Menthon, Custodian of the Privy Seal, sent Schuman word to come.

The story goes that when an emissary of the State Prosecutor arrived at City Hall in Metz with a warrant for Schuman's arrest as a suspected collaborator, the local police chief told him that M. Schuman could not be disturbed as he was at an important meeting of the Liberation Committee. Finally, the Minister in charge of Internal Security, Monsieur de Menthon, who was a member of the newly formed MRP which had recruited a variety of political groupings, (including Schuman's *Parti Démocrate Populaire* of pre-war days) had the charges against Schuman "filed', as none of them could be substantiated. Schuman received his political clearance just in time to register his candidature for his old constituency of Moselle in the election of October 21st, 1945 to the first Constituent Assembly. There he carried his seat with 103,264 votes. In the next election, which was for a new Parliament of the Fourth Republic, he increased his votes to 115,705. He held his seat until 1958, the year he retired from politics at the age of seventy-two.

A short while after he had arrived at Evrange, Metz was liberated and Robert Schuman was acclaimed as a leading citizen and as member of Parliament for the Metz constituency. He was also immediately appointed a member of the Liberation Committee which administered the shattered life of the city.

Thus little more than a year after he was attacked by the Paris government as a "collaborator" through the pressure of his political enemies, (who were either Gaullists or Communists) Schuman was not only back in Paris as a member of the Constituent Assembly, but was immediately entrusted with a vital Cabinet portfolio as Minister of Finance in the First Cabinet. By November 1947 he became France's third Prime Minister, succeeding the Socialist, Léon Blum, whose government lasted a few days less than a month and Paul Ramadier, who as a Radical had managed to hold his Cabinet together for about eight months.

Like Adenauer and De Gasperi, Schuman had no political party structure left to build on after the war. His *Parti Démocrate Populaire* no longer existed, as it had been merged into the MRP. Only the Communists, Socialists and Radicals had emerged into the post-war era in France with party cadres still intact, although the latter had been undermined by a number of its leaders who had subscribed to Munich and survived under Vichy. On the other hand the Radicals were helped by such formidable party leaders, returning from German captivity, as Edouard Herriot, and by others who had been prominent in the Resistance movement.

The *Mouvement Républicain Populaire*, better known as the MRP, which Schuman joined, was an improvisation containing all sorts of groups and combinations of various political and ideological backgrounds. The moderate Robert Schuman rapidly became the object of considerable distrust on the part of rabid Nationalists such as Georges Bideault, the leader of the MRP, and a number of others who felt that this man from Lorraine seemed more interested in peace than in reprisals. However, his firm convictions and clear political objectives soon made him not only a leader within his own newly constituted party affiliation, but a great figure who achieved much on the international scene.

CHAPTER VI

A Vacuum to be Filled

WHEN the smoke of battle and of smouldering rubble had somewhat settled I was sent from my post as managing director of the British United Press, which was headquartered in Montreal, to visit some of the territory I managed for the United Press as head of the European department before the war. Plans were being implemented to rebuild facilities disrupted and destroyed by war.

Probably the most forceful reality which seemed to stand out on close examination was the destruction, exhaustion and political confusion in Western Europe. It faced the hostility of the powerful and purposeful Soviet military and political machine, which was directed equally against former foes and allies. This fact, even if not yet apparent on the surface, seemed to intertwine the interests of the Western victors and vanquished to a remarkable degree.

Between lay a political vacuum, stretching from the Pyrenees to the Elbe river and from the North Sea to the Mediterranean and the Bosphorus. The phrase "political vacuum" is used advisedly, because there were neither political parties nor political organisations: not even the political structures of former parliamentary regimes remained.

In France, the combination of the *Front Populaire* government of the Third Republic and the final betrayal of France by the French Communists, who had sided with Stalin and Hitler for the first two years of the war until Hitler attacked Stalin, had destroyed the pre-war parliamentary structure of France beyond hope of restoration.

Since the French Revolution and the subsequent Directorate, France had twice been an empire, had been restored once as a kingdom under the Orléans and had three times become a republic. These regimes had succeeded one another to the accompaniment of more or less violent military upheavals at home and abroad. To restore France, therefore, the immediate question was: which France? She was technically, but only technically, among the victor countries. Those who saw France after the so-called liberation, after de Gaulle's triumphant entry into Paris in the wake of the United States and British troops, could have no doubt that the country was on the brink of disaster. Not only was Communism emerging in strength from the maquis. France was on the verge of psychological surrender to despondency and disunity bred by military defeat, by Nazi occupation and by her liberation more at the hands of the British-American forces than by her own military effort.

In Germany National Socialism had achieved a complete annihilation of parliamentary government, as it existed before the advent of Hitler. It would be giving Hitler too much credit to say that he destroyed the Weimar Republic. His advent and rise to power were symptoms as much of the inner political weakness of the German parliamentary regime as of the emergence of a new political ideology.

Many years before, Benito Mussolini had established Fascism in Italy, not as a political party but as a totalitarian State. The march on Rome and take-over of the government occurred in October, 1922. Over twenty years of totalitarian rule, including a victorious war in Ethiopia and a military defeat after World War II, had left the political structure of Italy, a country unified less than sixty years before the advent of Fascism, also a vacuum. True, it was still technically a monarchy and the monarch symbolised continuity of government, but it was a pale symbol, since in fact the allied military government was in control.

It is worth remembering that in 1918, when the Kaiser abdicated, Germany was left in very bad shape economically and politically, but the immediate transition to a republican regime with which the allies began negotiations secured the uninterrupted transfer of the Kaiser's sovereignty to another German state based on existing parliamentary political parties. The same applied to Austria after Emperor Charles had abdicated. After World War II, however, the only orderly transition from war to peace took place in Japan, where the continued reign of Emperor Hirohito, and the function of the Japanese parliament, allowed a much more natural resumption of industry and civilian order, despite the destruction wrought by the first atom bombs. It was in the heart of Europe that totalitarian rule was followed by total political vacuum.

This was only partly due to physical destruction on an unprecedented scale which had obliterated more than homes and factories. Germany in particular was politically and administratively paralysed. The life of modern communities ceases when all civilian government is eliminated. All civil servants and public employees down to the rank of the municipal dog-catcher were forbidden to follow their calling until they had submitted to a process of de-nazification. In totalitarian regimes every functionary automatically becomes a cog in a vast bureaucratic machine, especially in wartime. By not only eliminating the government, but also proclaiming a ban on all the civil servants, the cogs that have functioned in the totalitarian machine, modern society simply grinds to a halt. Since the totalitarian regimes, which had been in power for ten years in Germany and for thirty in Italy, were able completely to eliminate all political opposition, by police measures, the hangman's noose, the executioner's axe, the assassin's bullet, the firing squad, or the more modern means of scientific murder in gas chambers, the transition from one regime to another which was possible in vanquished countries in 1918 was not possible after World War II. Actually many countries, like Latvia, Lithuania, Poland and Austria, had even ceased to exist as sovereign States.

Also, 1945 was unlike 1918, when the victorious Western Allies faced a defeated Central Europe, in that in the latter year it was not a case of filling an absolute political, economic and social vacuum and rehabilitating a Continent.

In 1918, Eastern Europe was utterly self-absorbed in a murderous civil war which for years was to eliminate Russia as a political factor. In 1945 it was no longer a political no-man's land stretched across Russia and Siberia to the Pacific Ocean. In 1945 there was a Soviet military power (second only to the military might of the United States), straining to fill the political vacuum in China, Japan, Germany and Italy; for the first time this power had at its disposal a new political weapon, in the form of the Fifth Column of world Communism which was amply supplied with the financial wealth of Soviet gold, and which had built up an incredibly efficient apparatus for infiltrating the councils of the Western allies, not least into those of Washington and London.

First came the sensational revelations of the cypher clerk in the Soviet Embassy in Ottawa, Igor Gouzenko.[1] Copies of documents he turned over to the Canadian security police uncovered a vast espionage network in North America and Britain. It led to the arrest and conviction of such nuclear scientists as Nunn May and Klaus Fuchs as well as a number of key personnel in the United States and Canada. Other revelations centred on the United States government where Stalin had his trusted informers in the highest positions, such as for example Alger Hiss and the British diplomats stationed in Washington, Burgess and MacLean. One recalls the frightening revelations of the master Soviet spy in charge of vital British intelligence services, Kim Philby.[2]

The West's most sensitive areas of diplomacy, defence and strategic

[1] *This was my Choice*, Igor Gouzenko (Palm Publishers, 1948).
[2] *Philby—The Spy who Betrayed a Generation*, Page, Litch and Knightley (André Deutsch, London).

planning, in economic as well as scientific fields, were honey-combed by Moscow's devoted agents, motivated by political convictions so strong as to make the betrayal of their own countries appear virtuous in their eyes. Some of the facts would have challenged the most daring writer of spy fiction both by their ramifications and daring. But more baffling was the aspect of zeal and devotion to a political cause which was so novel that Western counter-espionage was utterly unprepared and incapable of coping with it—at first. It rendered resistance to Moscow's expansion into once free countries extremely difficult and often futile, as millions of once free non-Russians were being imprisoned for decades in the straight-jacket of communist dictatorships behind the Iron Curtain.

That the Iron Curtain failed to envelope all Europe was, judged in the political context of 1946, as great an achievement as the subsequent "economic miracle" of recovery in a number of once enemy countries which had borne the brunt of war's devastation.

The fear that gripped the Western allies when they realised what they faced in Soviet policy, was brought into the open for the first time in a memorable speech by Paul Henri Spaak, Belgium's dynamic Foreign Minister. On December 25th, 1949, at the first meeting of the United Nations in Paris at the Palais Chaillot, Russia's representative and Foreign Minister Victor Vishinsky attacked the Western allies for what he considered their hostile attitudes towards the Soviet Union. As Spaak recalls in his memoirs,[1] he pondered a while over Vishinsky's attacks and then decided to speak out frankly. On September 28th he took the floor and, addressing himself directly to the Soviet representative, said:

"What is the historic reality of these years? There is only one great nation which has emerged from the war having conquered the lands of others, and that nation is the USSR. It was during the war and for reasons of war you annexed the Baltic states. It was during the war and because of the war that you took a piece of Finland. It was during the war and because of the war that you took a piece out of Poland. It is because of your policies, impudent and vacillating, that you have today become all powerful in Warsaw, Prague, in Belgrade, in Bucharest and Sophia. It is because of your policy that you today occupy Vienna and that you occupy Berlin and that you do not seem to be prepared to abandon them. It is because of your policy that you today make claim to control the Ruhr. Your empire extends from the Black Sea to the Baltic and the Mediterranean. You would like to be on the shores of the Rhine, and then you ask us why we are concerned.

"The truth is that your foreign policy is more audacious and more

[1] *Combats Inachevés* (Fayard, Paris, 1969).

ambitious than that of the Tsars themselves. Finally, you maintain in each of the countries, here represented, a Fifth Column compared to which the Fifth Column of Hitler was but an organisation of Boy Scouts. There is not an area in the world, in Africa or Asia, which has difficulties or obstacles but you are there to increase them. That is your way of collaborating with the governments here represented, with whom you should be collaborating to assure peace. In each of our countries at this very moment there is a group of men who are not only your representatives and the defenders of your foreign policies (which in fact would not be very serious) but who do not miss an opportunity to weaken the state in which they live, politically, morally and socially".

Spaak's speech was punctuated by loud applause as he made point after point, and at the end of his attack it took the chairman over five minutes to bring under control the loud ovation given by the delegates of the Western countries to this man who obviously expressed feelings held by them all. Spaak noted in his autobiography that it was a satisfactory and a moving experience to find oneself the interpreter for a whole crowd, and to translate their hunger for peace and security into words.

Twenty years later Peking and Belgrade raised themselves against Moscow. Even Prague and Budapest struggled openly against Soviet repression as a prelude to the continuing erosion of Communist power, and Rumania angered its once unquestioned rulers by acclaiming no less a visitor than Richard Nixon, President of the United States.

The survival of a free Western Europe nursed the flickering flame of freedom in those areas the Red Army had occupied. The recovery of Western Europe, politically and economically, changed the faint flicker to a glow which was dangerous for Moscow's tyrants even among their own oppressed Russian people. This political development which occurred then, but whose repercussions will be shaping international politics for years to come, deserves closer examination.

It began in Italy, which ousted the dictator Mussolini and was the first Axis power to cease hostilities against the Allies. Italy had the oldest European history, and had been the cradle of European political development as the heir to Athens and the Caesars. From Italy the first organised governmental structures spread north with Roman conquests. It was in Italy that the city states, struggling against imperial power, first flourished as citizens' states. Italy had been and still in some respects remained, the crucible of political ideologies across the centuries.

After the fall of Mussolini, therefore, she became a political vacuum with every conceivable political heritage striving to establish itself with a vehemence of partisanship generated by centuries of division. Pivotal to the struggle in its various forms was the age-old historic rivalry between a strong central imperial government, which was the prerogative of a political state, and the claims of the individual who endeavoured to safeguard individual freedom by defending his local unit of city or country. No little influence on this struggle could be attributed to the presence of the papacy in Rome, where it had been engaged for well over a thousand years in defining what was God's and what was Caesar's.

Other nations of the Western world could look back on a mere few centuries of political disputes, never along such sharp lines of ideological demarcation as in Italy. In other countries there were personal rivalries between feuding rulers; in Italy these same rivalries involved Church and State, bringing to the fore yet more complicated ideological issues.

The ancient feuds between Guelphs and Ghibellines that raged in Italy were still discernible in the modern political line-ups, adding a particular fervour to disputes between the so-called clerical and anti-clerical trends which characterised most political parties, and which were born of centuries of tradition. There were other almost "hereditary" differences which strained unity within individual parties; for example, the Italian monarchists in Turin were loyal to the House of Savoy. But in the former kingdom of the Two Sicilies which included Naples and the South, the monarchist stronghold, that dynasty did not enjoy the same prestige as the Bourbons. When the plebiscite was called in 1946 to decide between monarchy and republic, many a southern monarchist cast his vote for a republic rather than vote for Savoy, which to them still meant Cavour and Garibaldi.

While De Gasperi was the man with the clearest general political concept and the profoundest social and political learning and philosophy, the most remarkable of the three men who came to the fore in creating a structure for political expression in the post-war period was Konrad Adenauer of Germany. In some ways the political odds against his country surviving political pressure from East and West, as well as economic catastrophe, were the highest. Like De Gasperi's, Adenauer's entry into politics following World War II, was accompanied by great hostility. We have already referred to the difficulties of Robert Schuman in France, who was able to manoeuvre successfully between the old-fashioned chauvinistic nationalism of General de Gaulle and his party president and political rival, Georges Bideault, on the one hand, and the destructively powerful influence of the resuscitated French Communist Party on the other.

These three men faced great odds. They were the targets of great suspicion on the part of Moscow, where their personal religious convictions were rightly seen as the determined enemy of the atheistic totalitarianism elevated by Moscow to a state religion. The Western Allies on the other hand were unwilling as yet to jeopardise their hopes of appeasing their erstwhile ally Joseph Stalin. London and Washington had every reason to fear the aggressive plans for world conquest of the Communist dictator in 1945, just as they had feared Hitler's aggressive plans for domination in 1935. But despite the proof of the disastrous effect political appeasement had as a reaction to fear in encouraging a dictator like Hitler, they were again courting trouble for many years to come when they repeatedly tried appeasing Moscow. Ceding to superior physical force is not appeasement. That is simply surrender. Appeasement always presupposes reasonable options. The most dangerous element here is when principles become so blurred that nothing seems worth fighting for.

This posed no problem to De Gasperi, Adenauer or Schuman, for they had been battling for their convictions since their early youth. These three men symbolised a fervent belief and had nothing more tangible behind them than just that when they ushered in a ten-year fight which will remain unique. In fact, during those years we saw the vanquished waging and winning a political battle to save the Western conquerors from their Eastern ally, by the establishment of a free Western Europe which hampered the course of Soviet expansion, and thus avoiding a war of mutual annihilation.

Chapter VII

The Struggle for Italy

It was De Gasperi's early conviction that the government to replace Mussolini should consist of individuals, rather than representatives of parties which in fact were no longer existent. All the parties had become virtual paper fictions with the possible exception of the Communists, whose leader Palmiro Togliatti, and some of his lieutenants had sought safety in Soviet Russia during the war and who had behind them both Russian funds and the powerful backing of Soviet Russia in the Allied Councils.

If party representation were to be accepted according to a key based on party strength more than twenty years earlier, that would have been the reassumption of an even greater fiction. No one knew as yet the true sentiment of the people on political principles. It would have been highly arbitrary. De Gasperi realised that if one did not accept the large number of Fascist seats held at the time by freely elected members of the Fascist party, any key would be misleading. Besides, how would an entirely new generation feel towards the old parties who had, after all, by their own weakness paved the way for Mussolini? But the Socialists and Communists refused to support a non-political Cabinet as proposed by De Gasperi: they wanted to establish their parties' existence rather than first face an election where their strength might not be as great as the new political force which was forming behind De Gasperi. In actual practice it turned out that the Cabinet before the elections was appointed from among political leaders, as De Gasperi had suggested. But the insistence on party labels also meant immediate party squabbles along doctrinaire lines rather than freedom for each member of the Cabinet to tackle problems according to the pragmatic judgments he might form as an individual.

This played primarily into the hands of the Communists. It permitted Togliatti to act, as he had a party which accepted his decisions which had been cleared with Moscow and not with any Italian caucus. As no party machine had yet actually been elected, however, other members of the Cabinet had immediately to submit to a self-appointed party council, which was arbitrarily constituted and not always too enlightened. This proved a considerable handicap to them as it left Togliatti, who knew that he had the confidence of Moscow, as the only member of that group able to rely on his own judgement.

The democratic parties, as well as the Western Allies, had already received a rude shock. The United States had indicated a desire to withdraw support from the King and his government of non-political caretakers under Marshal Badoglio. They preferred to encourage the Republicans who were led by Count Sforza, and the Neapolitan wing of the National Liberation Committee. This was presided over by Benedetto Croce, the well-known philosopher and historian who was an enemy of the House of Savoy. Washington wanted to refuse cooperation unless the King abdicated immediately, whilst London actually favoured a constitutional monarchy. To everybody's consternation and surprise, Moscow extended diplomatic recognition to King Victor Emanuel's regime: reluctantly and somewhat shamefacedly London and Washington had to follow the Communist lead. The political tactics of the Communists were a credit to the ability of Palmiro Togliatti, and a few years later he managed to split the Socialist Party on the question of Communist participation in the coalition government. When De Gasperi was able to oust the Communists from the government in 1947, he was supported by some Socialists led by Giuseppe Saragat. Most of the Socialists, however, followed the Socialist Party leader Pietro Nenni who with the Communists, in the name of Marxist solidarity, also left the government. It took years to heal that rift; Socialist unity was restored in 1963, only to face another disruption in 1969, when Nenni parted company with those Socialists who wanted, as Nenni had advocated earlier, the Communists back in a coalition government, and Nenni instead supported a coalition with the Christian Democrats.

No sooner had Moscow recognised the regime of the King, acting through Marshal Badoglio, than Palmiro Togliatti again outmanoeuvred the Socialist and other Left groups who had close contact with Western Socialist and Allied governments. Badoglio appointed the Liberal Ivanoe Bonomi to form a government, but the Socialist and Left voters refused to cooperate, as they were fearful of losing popular support in the face of initial intransigent opposition to Badoglio from the Communists. As soon as the Democratic Left refused to cooperate, Togliatti, who had meanwhile returned from Moscow under the assumed name of Ercole Ercoli, changed tactics and in April 1944 agreed to serve under Bonomi. He argued that in accordance with the policy dictated by Moscow it was necessary "to renew political life in Italy even in co-operation with the king and Badoglio". Having thus outmanoeuvred his own Marxist rivals, he demanded an important post in the new government and his party became a key influence in the Bonomi cabinet. For Moscow the prime issue was not "unconditional surrender", as the Western Allies under Franklin Roosevelt's tutelage were insisting, but to keep the Italians in the war under any government, as long as they continued to harass the Germans who were still pressing hard on the Soviet front.

The Western Allies had lost much precious time between the Italian offer to surrender and the actual signing of the Armistice. From the voluminous literature of the time it seems fairly obvious that the theoreticians among the U.S. negotiators, and the old political resentment felt by the British against their Italian colonial rivals of the past, were sufficient to blind them all to the political reality emerging in post-war Europe. Both nations could see that "unconditional surrender", even at best, needed methods of implementation. What the Italians proposed as methods of avoiding chaos, the Americans misunderstood as conditions, while the British were disinterested in any possibility of Italy, even without Mussolini, eventually making a come-back as their rival in the Mediterranean, or worse still, developing rival colonial ambitions in Africa. While protracted armistice negotiations were going on in Lisbon, the Germans had an opportunity to re-organise their still formidable military forces, in Italy itself. Thus time was provided to establish a German army of occupation in effective military control of Italy.

Negotiations were commenced in Lisbon with the Allies in August 1943, and it took about two months of footling back-and-forth, as the Allies feared that Italy was trying to obtain too favourable a treatment. When General Castelano finally signed the Armistice in Cassibile on September 3rd, the Germans were ready, and on September 9th their troops marched into Rome.

Not only did this delay permit the German troops to regroup, but it also gave them a chance to kidnap Mussolini, who had been hidden away by the Badoglio Directorate in the Gran Sasso region.

In fact, before long, the Italian suggestions which had at first been refused by the Allies had to be accepted as facts of life. In his study, *The Political History of Post-War Italy*,[1] Norman Kogan pointed out that a revival of civil and military activities in Italy was entirely dependent on Allied supplies. But the British, for the reasons already given, were particularly afraid of Italian rehabilitation and showed great intransigence in their dealings with the men of the National

[1] Frederick A. Praeger, New York.

Liberation Committee (*Comitato Liberazione Nazionale*), especially with De Gasperi and Count Sforza. This for a while threatened the tenuous prestige necessary to these men if they were to replace the Fascists with authority in the eyes of their own countrymen. Finally, on September 26th, from New York, a joint British-U.S. Declaration assured anti-Fascist Italy of some assistance. In the intervening three weeks the country had been brought to the verge of starvation, for the Germans had cut off all supplies and the Allies had not yet decided how to cope with the situation. Having issued this Declaration from Hyde Park, Roosevelt (outwitted by Moscow in his dealings with the Badoglio government) also announced his readiness to exchange ambassadors with the new regime. But Britain still refused to follow suit, making the United States hesitate and again causing delay. Then new difficulties arose in the battle to clear the peninsula of Germans. Could Italy be given some sort of military potential? Here obstruction came from France, Yugoslavia, Greece and Albania, who had all suffered Italian military action and were most reluctant to see the revival of military power in Italy. In May, 1945 Yugoslavia invaded and occupied Trieste and large parts of the surrounding area; French troops violated the lines drawn by the Allies in 1944, and in April 1945 de Gaulle gave orders to the French army to occupy areas of Piedmont and the Valle d'Aosta. It was only after the bluntest of threats addressed to de Gaulle by President Truman, to cut off all supplies to the French army, that de Gaulle yielded and finally withdrew his troops in July of the same year. Marshal Tito of Yugoslavia was harder to dislodge.

The publicity given to Allied discords permitted the phantom republic of Salo, which Mussolini had in the meantime set up with German arms in North Italy, to derive a semblance of short lived political attention.

De Gasperi had been named Minister without portfolio in the first cabinet constituted by the King and Badoglio in 1944. He represented (as was later shown by the first elections), the largest section of public opinion in Italy. His followers accepted his clearly enunciated beliefs based on Christian concepts, guaranteeing personal liberty and respect for individual dignity. But De Gasperi had as yet no political structure and hence was not even entrusted with a portfolio. The second strongest group consisted of the Communists, who had openly sided with Soviet Russia in the rising friction with the Western Allies. The curious fact remained that it was due to the Western Allies that Togliatti had established the strength of the Communist party. They had first provided buildings and facilities for the Communists as part of their programme for the restoration of "democratic representatives", and then hoisted him into political prominence, by handicapping Sforza and De Gasperi, his opponents.

De Gasperi's astounding achievement will remain a political phenomenon which students of contemporary history will continue to examine for years to come, and his victory rightly has been hailed as decisive for the Free World.

The big factor against De Gasperi was that his chief opponent, Palmiro Togliatti, emerged from the war with a political machine vastly strengthened by the overwhelming prestige of Soviet Russia, Russian gold and the facilities turned over to the Communists by the Western Allies in the form of the Fascist Party Headquarters, and even allied military appointments to mayoralities which were key positions for electoral purposes in Italy.

A mortal struggle for Italy, holder of the key political position in Europe, then began between De Gasperi and Togliatti. In the second Bonomi government De Gasperi assumed the portfolio of Foreign Minister. Italy had no real international relations as yet, and De Gasperi was faced with the immense task of convincing the Allies that his struggle to establish democracy in the face of Moscow's blandishments was the immediate concern of the whole of the Western World to whom the immediate possibility of Italy's acceptance of the bait was as much a threat to it as to Italy herself.

When finally the first post-war elections came, De Gasperi, without a real party organisation or funds which could remotely compare with the money available to Togliatti and the facilities available to the Socialists (who could draw on some very substantial support from the British Labour Party), obtained 35.2 per cent of the popular vote. But the Marxists, Communists and Socialists together, gathered 40 per cent. Only when the Socialists under Giuseppe Saragat broke away from Socialist leader Pietro Nenni, who wanted his Socialist Party to cooperate with the Communists, was the Communist-Socialist block reduced to 35 per cent of the votes, the 5 per cent who were followers of Giuseppe Saragat throwing in their lot with De Gasperi in an anti-Communist coalition cabinet. None of the many other parties could muster even 10 per cent of the votes. The Liberals who were the leading pre-war party, obtained 6.8 per cent while a strange post-war "common man's party" (*l'Uomo Qualunque*) of definite neo-Fascist tendencies secured 5.3 per cent.

But the battle against the Communists still had to be fought on two planes, domestic and international. At home De Gasperi had won the support of his people in the votes of many and the respect of more. But internationally it was an uphill struggle. The account[1] of De Gasperi's first trip to London makes pathetic reading. While still serving

[1] *De Gasperi Nella Politica Estera Italiana* (Mondadori, Milan).

De Gasperi, his secretary and close collaborator, Paolo Canali, described it in a book published under the pseudonym, "Adstans".

When De Gasperi landed in a military airplane at Finchley Airport in London on September 18th, 1945, it was the first visit of an Italian Cabinet Minister after the war, and the first official contact with the Allies to discuss peace terms. The immediate object of the trip was to present Italy's case against Yugoslavia. De Gasperi came to plead for a return of Trieste and Venezia Giulia, unilaterally occupied by Yugoslav troops. Long before the Western Allies had terminated their relationship, and in some cases intimate friendship with Mussolini, De Gasperi had been exposed to great peril in his opposition to the dictator. But, ". . . how many humiliations were to be experienced by the Italians who had been invited to appear (at the conference) with an advance notice of only thirty-six hours", Canali writes. "The icy atmosphere reserved for ex-enemy aliens began to make itself felt already at the airport, where the Minister of Foreign Affairs (De Gasperi) and his companions were not spared the tiresome line-up at the Customs and the interminable questioning by immigration officials in time of war".

"Finally De Gasperi sat down on the wooden bench in front of the agent of the Immigration Service. "How long do you expect to remain in England?" asked the agent of the Foreign Minister, when he had finished going through a series of routine questions. "The shortest possible time", was the response one of the staff (Paolo Canali) replied in English for the Foreign Minister." As Canali recounted to me years later, it was the most mortifying and humiliating reception for a Foreign Minister and for a man of the calibre and achievements of De Gasperi, and was so undeserved as to appear calculated.

"The icy reception and the uncertain immediate future were the reasons De Gasperi immersed himself even more in his own thoughts, which were by no means happy ones", wrote Canali. As Sir Noel Charles, the British Ambassador to Italy picked up De Gasperi in his large official car at the Immigration Station to drive him to London, he attempted no conversation, not even polite chit-chat to relieve the frigid and friendless reception.

When they arrived at Lancaster House, where the conference was to take place, the indignities were not yet at an end. As the Foreign Minister of Yugoslavia, Kardeljy, had apparently suffered discomfort during the flight from Belgrade to London, he was late. Since De Gasperi was the next speaker after Kardeljy, he was not allowed into the conference hall but had to sit in a waiting room all afternoon and all morning the next day, till the Yugoslav had recovered from his air-sickness. The bitterness of the situation did not escape the other members of the Italian group, and De Gasperi, as he ascended the stairs for the third time into the now familiar antechamber, commented that humiliation was meted out to those least responsible for this Nemesis: "The mortification of this road to Canossa really belongs to others".

Chapter VIII

Filling the German Vacuum

The United States, like the other Allies (particularly the Soviets), had been busy for years compiling lists of individuals, categorising them into "war criminals", Nazis of varying intensity, as politically reliable or unreliable, to be used or jailed once Hitler had been ousted. Those designated on U.S. lists as "white" could be used for civilian duties in a conquered Germany. Konrad Adenauer was at the top of the "white list" of those who had impeccable records during the Nazi years. When the Americans occupied the city of Cologne, Adenauer as "White Number One" on the American list,[1] was sought out by the U.S. military and charged with resuming his duties as Chief Magistrate of the City of Cologne.

Adenauer made it clear that he was only willing to act as consultant to the American Commanding Officer, but not to assume responsibility, since he was merely empowered to submit his opinions to the military rulers, not to act upon them. Adenauer was then driven from his villa in Roehndorf to Cologne where Lt. Col. Robert Hyles was Military Commander of the half of the city under Allied control. German troops were still holding out in pockets of resistance on the right bank, and the city was then eighty per cent destroyed (it was still largely a rubble heap when I visited it in 1946). When Adenauer was asked to exercise the consultant's duties of Mayor, only 32,000 remained out of a normal pre-war population of some 760,000 inhabitants, and there was not sufficient housing even for them. Only 300 houses remained undamaged in the entire city. There was no food, no fuel, no water system, no sewers or essential sanitation services. Thousands of corpses lay putrefying under the rubble. As I later saw in cities such as Würzburg, Nürnberg and Munich, the people of Cologne in 1945 were living mainly in cellars. They were cooking with wooden debris on improvised barrel stoves, and spent all day scrounging something to cook. The task confronting the re-instituted Mayor of the once proud imperial city

[1] *Letters of Lieutenant Colonel Patterson*, C.A.R. to Col. Geary, XXII Corps, APO 250. U.S. Army of May 8, 1945.

he had governed from 1917 to 1933 was formidable. Despite the greatest cooperation received from an extremely generous U.S. military government, the physical problems of restoring even a semblance of order to the ruined city took more than ordinary determination and tenacity.

As Adenauer wrote in his memoirs: "The Allies had come to the conclusion that the strength of the German people to resist would be most severely weakened by the destruction of their homes and their houses. The Allies had further reached the conclusion that mass attacks with thousands of planes would best break the morale of the civilian population. This is why the systematic destruction of civilian residential areas was undertaken."[1]

As a war measure it proved a debatable tactic on purely technical grounds, and for building a better future, particularly as an effective antidote to Hitler's brutalities, it was political folly and set a dangerous precedent. That is why Golo Mann wrote: "The European order which the Allies had wanted to save was not after all restored in 1945, and to that extent the war had been in vain. For six years his (Hitler's) enemies had tried to satisfy Hitler; then for six years they had shot and thrown bombs in order to get rid of him. This they achieved, but not much else."[2] However, with the full support of the U.S. Army, Adenauer tackled the formidable task and slowly began to revive a dead city.

Then the work of reconstruction was suddenly interrupted. Cologne became part of the British Zone of Occupation, and the U.S. military turned the area over to the British Commander on June 21st, 1945. Friction began almost on their entry. Adenauer, as he wrote in his memoirs, felt the treatment of the civilian population became unnecessarily harsh. But above all, political tension was generated within weeks after the July elections in Britain. The Labour Party, now in power in England, wanted to impose a socialist regime on the Germans. Clement Attlee did everything, through the military government, to aid Kurt Schumacher, the German Socialist leader and Konrad Adenauer's political opponent. All co-operation between Adenauer and the military government came to a halt.

The lengths to which the British Labour government went were remarkable. They immediately established cooperation between the British Intelligence Service and the German Socialist Party to report against Schumacher's rivals. The Socialist City Administrator, Robert Goerlinger, who became a sort of political mentor to the

[1] *Erinnerungen—1945–1953,* Konrad Adenauer (DVA–Stuttgart) page 25–English Frederick Praeger, New York.

[2] *The History of Germany since 1789* Golo Mann, (Chatto & Windus, London), page 466.

British army, began to furnish the Intelligence Service with lengthy reports on proceedings at the City Hall, which were later part of the archives at Adenauer's disposal when he became Chancellor. He quotes from them at length, showing the unfavourable light cast upon his own actions.

One of the first areas of conflict with the military government was Adenauer's opposition to wholesale application of denazification proceedings.

On May 31st Winston Churchill sent a message to the Secretary of War and to General Ismay, *For Chiefs of Staff*, in which he said: "The Minister of Agriculture tells me that there is no hope for adequate food production next year in Germany, unless the present order of the Combined Chiefs of Staff to General Eisenhower to arrest all members of the Reich Food Board is cancelled. This order was framed before we entered Germany. It was based on the assumption that all German officials concerned were virulent Nazis. Individual officials should be judged on their record, as in the case of other German industries".

But Churchill's repeated warnings, directed towards getting things moving again, were disregarded by his successor Attlee. Hence Adenauer was faced with incalculable difficulties. From letter-carriers to garbage collectors, not to mention City Hall clerks and engineers, everyone had been forced to join the Nazi labour or professional organisations, irrespective of political background, merely in order to maintain their livelihood. To force denazification on everybody who had been in any way part of the Nazi structure, meant dismissing practically the entire civil population and paralysing the city. In the U.S. and French Zones a civilian had to defend himself against concrete accusations of Nazi criminal activities: the British insisted that the individual had to prove his innocence rather than disprove his guilt, a requirement completely contrary to British legal practice.

It must be remembered that as yet no clear definition of guilt had been given. "In my eyes", Adenauer wrote, "it was essential to examine each individual case. Heroism (in defying Hitler) is not a daily commonplace". Considering his record, the British could not very well suspect Adenauer of Nazi leanings and he pleaded for a less rigid application of the law, simply to get the city services and administration going again. But the British resented this, and Adenauer was attacked as politically unreliable.

This crucial matter, on which Adenauer took a firm stand, proved an important point in the rising tension between himself and Brigadier Barraclough, Military Governor of the North Rhine Province, obviously acting under direct orders of the Socialist government in London. While the question was in suspense some British journalists arrived, and hearing of the discussion they approached the Lord Mayor for his opinion.

As Lord Mayor of Cologne in the First World War (1918) Adenauer had begun, with the cooperation of the British Military Governor, to plant a green belt of trees around the city to replace dismantled fortifications, this being considered necessary to safeguard the health of the population of this crowded industrial centre. In September 1945, Adenauer suddenly received orders from the British to cut down all the trees of the green belt for fuel. Actually the firewood thus obtained would have been but a drop in the ocean, and meant much less than the release of a train-load of coal from the Ruhr, which was easily available to the army for these purposes while the deleterious effect on the health of the population during the years needed to grow a new tree belt was entirely out of proportion to the amount of fuel involved.

In an interview with the *News Chronicle* of London, Adenauer's frank answers to questions regarding his attitude aroused attention. A few days later he was requested to appear before Brigadier Barraclough in the latter's office. This time he was refused a chair while the Brigadier, sitting at his desk, sternly read a twelve point indictment of Adenauer for insubordination. He then dismissed him from his post as mayor, and prohibited any public utterance and all participation in public and political activity. This would have effectively eliminated Adenauer as a rival of the Socialist Kurt Schumacher. Adenauer was then asked to sign a document admitting the accusations and accepting the order to desist from political activity. He answered with a short, sharp "Nein!", turned on his heel and left. As he went, Barraclough threatened him with arrest, should there be the least breach of his orders. Years later, as German Federal Chancellor, Adenauer met Brigadier Barraclough at an official dinner and was asked what his thoughts had been when dismissed from his post. "At home I have a document, "Dismissed by the Nazis'. I shall now draw up another document, 'Dismissed by the Liberators' ", Adenauer replied.

With the ousting of Adenauer, the British thought that by muzzling him, they had cleared the political road for their protégé, Kurt Schumacher. Actually, the reverse was true. Travelling beyond the military jurisdiction of the Cologne commander, he now had time to begin organising the Christian Democrat Party.

CHAPTER IX

Schuman's Challenge to France

WE have already seen how Robert Schuman had to dodge his own French police, to avoid being liquidated by de Gaulle. It is curious to note that de Gaulle once approached Schuman, offering him membership in his own RPF party, no doubt sensing the political possibilities represented by a man of Schuman's firm convictions. When Schuman refused, mainly because of de Gaulle's nationalism, the General apparently singled him out for special attacks which became vehement during the launching of the Schuman Plan.

Schuman himself was starting anew. He had not only lost his pre-war party, which had been absorbed into the MRP, but the MRP rightly described itself as a movement, not a party, because it was in the throes of serious internal dissensions on matters of foreign policy, while holding the middle line in domestic affairs. Backed by a substantial number of influential members, Georges Bideault, its president, was at first closer to de Gaulle and his nationalistic leanings. Both advocated the partition of Germany, closer ties with Moscow to counter-balance Anglo-United States influence and, by the same token, were opposed to a European union, unless under French hegemony and not as backed by the United States.

But even more serious was the fact that Robert Schuman, in advocating European understanding, was not merely challenging de Gaulle and Bideault: he was challenging a classic tenet of political faith which had been France's guiding emotion since Napoleon I.

It is necessary to put his struggles in context to appreciate fully what Schuman had to face and what he eventually achieved.

Early in May, 1946 I had embarked from New York on the *S.S. Brazil,* which was at that time still a military transport but no longer used for troops. She carried mainly a vast army of civilian administrators, the so-called "Columbia Gauleiters", men trained largely at Columbia University or other U.S. establishments for civilian administration of conquered countries. I happened to share a cabin with a detachment of grave-diggers, who were destined for the macabre task of exhuming and identifying dead U.S. soldiers.

There were also groups of German and French political exiles and an assortment of black-marketeers labelled mostly as "social workers" or just "re-educators". It was as interesting a passenger list as one could wish, and I was able to see at close quarters how a return to Europe at that time brought one into the closest contact with the improvised peace which was to follow a carefully planned war.

When I looked round at my travelling companions I felt it was symbolic of the wider situation to find that apart from a number of earnest, idealistic and devoted men and women, who were prepared to do their best in the appalling situation of destruction, hunger, disease and dire poverty, there were a certain number of characters who obviously felt that the lawlessness that accompanies all social chaos held considerable promise for fishing in muddy waters.

Prepared to see and learn details about the big issues confronting the world, I was rapidly brought up short by the very human reactions of single individuals living in a restricted area and seeing everything in terms of their own immediate surroundings, personal experiences and needs. In an age when one hears so much of the group, the collective, the community, the mass and society, it came almost as a surprise to see how the individual seems to encapsulate himself mentally and psychologically. The larger the issues involved, the more it seemed that the centre of interest for each individual with whom I came in contact in various countries at that time was merely his or her shrinking *Umwelt*, his tangible day-to-day experiences. It made me realise that as society gets more collectivised, the individual seems to retreat more into himself and his own world. As the individual increasingly realises his impotence to influence events which baffle him, he feels that his only option left is to opt out, which today goes by that somewhat meaningless word "alienation".

In half bombed-out Cherbourg or completely bombed-out Munich, walking through the rubble in Nürnberg or Hamburg or observing the misery of post-war disorganisation in Rome, I was amazed to see how self-centred and preoccupied people were with their immediate problems. They were surprisingly disinterested in the great issues for which their armies had fought and remarkably vague and apathetic about their political future. Much of this disinterestedness was obviously caused by the dire need and privations they were and had been experiencing. And yet I could not help noticing there was an amazingly strong will to survive, to clear the rubble and to restore normality. So much of what had happened to these people in the last twenty years, whether in France, Germany or Italy, was really incomprehensible to them. It was the work of governments which they looked upon as remote, uncontrollable, and hence, inevitable, the consequence of actions in which they felt themselves in no way personally involved. In Italy and Germany free franchise had not existed, but its survival in France had not saved her from succumbing to dictators, and foreign ones at that. One seems to sense a very ancient reaction in the suffering of people. For centuries they had passively fallen victim to the whims of princes, the violence of their lords or their rivals, to wars, pestilence and hunger, which they regarded partly as acts of God and partly as inevitable misfortunes, conjured up by evil men.

I spoke with men who had been in concentration camps, and who had suffered greatly. A certain atrophy of interest in wider questions sets in, they told me, as they withdraw from wider reality and thereby permit themselves to survive mentally, and maybe also physically as the monotonous rhythm of prison routine and suffering lasts and lasts and lasts.

This seems to explain why a great deal of talk regarding the restoration of free franchise under democratic parliamentary regime did not evoke the expected response in people liberated from totalitarian rule. It was not government machinery that interested them, but the men who control it, and this in turn accounted for the emergence of De Gasperi, Adenauer and Schuman.

When I arrived in France, an election campaign[1] had just been launched. In a dispatch to the Union Press I mentioned as the outstanding development the vehemence with which the Socialists were now attacking their coalition partners, the Communists. Maurice Thorez, the Communist leader, was being singled out for direct personal attacks which were led by the Socialist Minister of the Interior, Letroquer, in which he castigated Thorez as a war dodger, a deserter and a foreign quisling now returned from Moscow to assume the role of potential dictator. This did not prevent General de Gaulle from extending an amnesty and taking Thorez into his government.

Against both Marxist parties stood the moderate Republican party *MRP—Mouvement Républicain Populaire*) advocating a Christian Social democracy at home. Its main support came from the vast white-collar proleteriat, wage earners and intellectuals, university students in the large cities and the professional and merchant middle class.

Misery was the greatest single domestic factor, hunger more potent than ideology, survival of the individual more immediate than a

[1] Election of June 2, 1946

party's future. The election campaign, with all its bitterness and political rivalries, had to be fought on a very simple platform, the simplest common denominator, namely food. Even the Communists were coming in for a great deal of criticism from their own French rank and file. Since their leader Maurice Thorez was playing a prominent part in the first Cabinet at the time, he was also being accused by his own party members of neglect of the immediate problems.

At the time of writing my first dispatches from Paris, the butchers had not received fresh meat for two weeks. Many districts in the country were worse off. One interesting item I reported at the time was a politically very effective story circulated as an election rumour by the opposition to the government, namely that the meat was short because it was being shipped off to England. Britain's popularity was as low as that of the United States, to both of whom France owed its liberation.

I recall one example of simple food propaganda the Communists used for electioneering purposes while I was in Paris. It was most effective and entirely fraudulent. There was an appalling shortage of bread, and Bogomolov, the Soviet Ambassador to Paris, invited the press and a trainload of prominent people to Marseilles to welcome a Soviet grain ship. The Communist press gave out the story that the United States and Canadian grain was being shipped to Bremen to feed the Germans, while Soviet Russia was giving of her own meagre supplies to the French. These "meagre supplies" arrived in Marseilles from the Black Sea port of Odessa with great fanfare and extensive press coverage throughout France. Madame Bogomolov received a large bouquet of red roses from the Mayor of Marseilles with "gratitude to the Soviet people", while sacks of grain were being unloaded. A little later, however, it was discovered that the grain Russia had shipped to Marseilles had been shipped in the same sacks from Canada to the Soviet port of Odessa, under the Allied aid programme to Soviet Russia. In Odessa it was trans-shipped to a Soviet vessel and brought to France for propaganda purposes. The grain had cost Russia nothing, except the hunger of her own people deprived of this gift from Canada and the U.S.A. while this Western aid to Soviet Russia was now paying political dividends by stirring up anti-Western sentiment. Moreover, as the Russians were no doubt aware, publication of this fraud was unwelcome to the Western governments at that time, anxious as they were not to offend Russia.

Russia repeated this crude deception in other countries, including her own satellites, and particularly in Italy. The political confusion, I noted in my dispatches, led to an early emergence of a strong trend towards the leadership principle, the so-called personality cult in France.

In the introduction to his History of the Fourth Republic[1] Jacques Fauvet attributes the end of the fourth in the series of French republican regimes to what has often been called, "bonapartism". He describes it as a periodic fever induced by "explosive mixtures: a combination of an appeal to the little man and a call for the big soldier", recalling that since the French Revolution two emperors were followed by two marshals, two generals and one colonel. In this century alone, he says, there came to power Col. de la Rocque, 1934–36, Marshal Pétain 1939–42, and General de Gaulle, 1947–48 and again in 1953 (to 1969), and comments: "There are two things of singular inconstancy in France, feminine fashions and political popularity".

Books have been written about the strange French political phenomenon, and the constant clash between radical and traditional ideas. Historians will have ample material to work on, much confusion to clarify and many contradictions to reconcile in writing the history of France in modern times. In fact, to understand modern France one has to go back to the French Revolution of 1789.

Through the years that followed, mainly under Napoleon I, France accepted a European idea in principle, but only under French hegemony. If she could not rule, she was determined to oppose all other efforts at joint solution. In modern times she at first refused to cooperate in the Hoover Moratorium of 1931, when Europe including France was on the brink of bankruptcy. Again she resisted the Marshall Plan in 1947. The negative role of de Gaulle in unifying efforts towards European political federation, the common European defence and the common market, is in line with an old tradition. To add to the paradox, while Frenchmen elected governments opposed to closer integration of interests, France produced great intellects and pioneers to lead Europe. In the thirties there was Aristide Briand; foremost among them after World War II came Robert Schuman and Jean Monet.

France was created a modern centralised state by the love of grandeur and competent aggressiveness of Napoleon Bonaparte. He achieved what Louis XIV had striven for but failed to realise in his heirs. Napoleon the conqueror unleashed the spirit of Messianic vocation in France, and it was this very "esprit de grandeur" which Charles de Gaulle lived and re-lived, a ghost of past glories. Vainly he tried to incarnate in himself a grandiose future to atone for France's dismal failures in the thirties. It had generated a psychosis

[1] *La Quatrième République* (Fayard).

of self-vindication in France from which Charles de Gaulle drew his strength.

In all this de Gaulle was not unlike Napoleon III who came to power against incredible odds. France had suffered military defeat at Leipzig in 1813 and again at Waterloo in 1815. Military occupation, humiliation and political disintegration had prepared the ground for one man to transform utter national frustration into nationalistic frenzy.

Accepted as a reincarnation of the past glories of his uncle Napoleon I, Louis Napoleon was elected to the Republican Parliament as a Republican deputy. Incredible as it seemed, in view of the mediocrity of the man, he was borne by a romantic people to the highest office of the Republic, that of President. Eventually he conspired with the army against the republic he had given his oath to defend, and ascended the throne of his uncle, Napoleon I, to have himself crowned Emperor Napoleon III in 1852.

In a biography of Napoleon III, the Italian Mario Mazzucchelli tells how the Emperor was preoccupied with the tremendous growth of the United States since the days when France had helped the former British colonies to gain their independence. In less than a hundred years from the Declaration of Independence, the new continent had assumed a position of supremacy which Napoleon III considered a possible danger for the Old World. He questioned what would happen when this people, grown rich by their own effort and therefore become powerful, one day used their battleships and merchant fleets to dominate Europe and to impose the products of their agriculture and industry upon the Old Continent. He believed that if he could create a Latin empire in Mexico, to counterbalance the new Anglo-Saxon power in North America, he could dissipate this danger. The obsession with which Charles de Gaulle pursued similar efforts, though with different means, whenever and wherever he could find an opportunity, is a matter of history.

Napoleon III had his Crimean War[1]. He had his vain dream of a Mexican empire to challenge the power of the United States and Britain's Indian empire by making Maximilian of Habsburg Emperor of Mexico and France's satellite. Shortly after the assassination of Lincoln and the assumption of the presidency by that rough diamond, Andrew Jackson, with his super nationalist Secretary of State, Seward, the French adventures in North America were rapidly challenged. Napoleon III yielded to Jackson's threat and abandoned Maximilian to face a Mexican firing squad[2]. He also extended the French Empire to Indo-China and Africa.

[1] 1854–1856.
[2] Shot at Queretaro, 1867, together with two of his generals.

Napoleon had a rude awakening from his dream when Bismarck defeated him at Sedan in 1870, and Queen Victoria is quoted as having referred to him as "that confused dreamer who is drawing himself and France into a disaster with the purposefulness of an obsessed sleepwalker. He is linking coming events and his own future destiny to the dream of a romantic". Napoleon's romantic dream of an Asian empire in the nineteenth century ended with the French defeat at Dien Bien Phu in the twentieth century, shortly before the return of de Gaulle. His African dreams were ended by de Gaulle in Algiers and Morocco.

While the events of de Gaulle's life followed a different sequence they nevertheless show certain parallels with events in the life of Napoleon III. The collapse of France under the first attacks from Hitler's Germany was a repetition of her defeat by the upstart Prussia at Sedan. Both Napoleon and de Gaulle were dreaming of a French nation in the Americas to "curb" the United States. De Gaulle mounted an attack on the U.S. dollar which failed, thereby weakening the French franc. He dreamt vainly of a "*Québec libre*" as a satellite, just as Napoleon had dreamt of a French satellite Hapsburg in Mexico. Both General de Gaulle and Napoleon III ruled a France which was trying to reassert herself after humiliations following upon her adventurous initiatives beyond her economic, military or even political capacity. For a nation to accept and elevate two such leaders within a century certainly supports Jacques Fauvet's contention that bonapartism is an occupational hazard of French politics, and the sentiments with which Winston Churchill and Roosevelt regarded de Gaulle are reminiscent of Queen Victoria's estimate of Napoleon III.

On October 21st, 1945 the first election to a constituent assembly took place, in the form of a plebiscite in which de Gaulle won handsomely on one issue with 96 per cent, and on the other with 66 per cent of the votes.

Despite de Gaulle's victory on referendum questions, the first elections also revived various political parties, whose members laid down conditions for their support. De Gaulle impatiently uttered warnings that the dismal party strife of the Third Republic was reviving under the Fourth. On January 21st, 1946 he called a cabinet meeting—significantly not as usual at the Hotel Matignon, the Prime Minister's residence, but at the War Office, of which de Gaulle was also the responsible minister. To a baffled and shocked Cabinet he declared that his job was complete and announced his intention to retire.

In his *Histoire de la Libération*[1] Robert Aron states that the General

[1] *Histoire de la Libération*, Robert Aron (Calman Levy, Paris).

had decided to retire as early as September 1944, and quotes him as saying, "I shall withdraw from government . . . one must disappear. France might yet need an untarnished image. One must conserve such an image for her. Jeanne d'Arc, had she married, would no longer have remained Jeanne d'Arc; one must disappear". This "untarnished image" reappeared on June 1st, 1958, when the National Assembly believed de Gaulle was the one person capable of re-establishing discipline in the army and the authority of a state on the brink of dissolution, a condition to which de Gaulle had himself greatly contributed. From his nominal retreat at Colombey-les-deux-Eglises, (which he left occasionally to make a speech or give a press conference in Paris or else where), he guided his followers in the RPF in the French Assembly in the gradual destruction of the Fourth Republic.

With the temporary disappearance of de Gaulle the MRP emerged as the strongest political faction, and Robert Schuman the strongest influence. His views won popular support.

The struggle between the Bideault nationalist trend and Robert Schuman's European ideas had remained unresolved for some time. Georges Bideault accepted Communist support in joint opposition to the Marshall Plan. Like de Gaulle, he constantly tried to rally Moscow support for French policies abroad, in an effort to thwart what he regarded as Anglo-Saxon efforts to rehabilitate Germany. Bideault had even tried secretly to baulk the efforts of Léon Blum, the Socialist leader, to reach economic agreement with the United States, securing U.S. loans for France. De Gaulle and Bideault later became bitter enemies (Bideault fleeing from France and returning only after de Gaulle's 1968 pre-election amnesty), despite the fact that they were together the strongest proponents of a dismembered Germany. Some, among them Jacques Fauvet, believed the feud began when Bideault "betrayed" Charles de Gaulle, at the time of de Gaulles's dramatic retirement announcement on January 21st, 1946. The General had not anticipated Bideault's support for a "political government" after his own retirement. Without the MRP's assistance, a majority would have been impossible, and de Gaulle had counted on being asked to return and reassume the government. Instead Bideault swung his party's support behind Felix Gouin of the Socialists, and in return received a Cabinet appointment. The chronic changes of government and final paralysis in 1958 led to the establishment of the Fifth Republic, the authoritarian regime of a strong executive and weakened legislature. But despite the rift between de Gaulle and Bideault, as late as June 1948 de Gaulle was urging a policy for France of "no more Reich". To him the Reich would automatically become a viable instrument to revive the German instinct for domination *a fortiori* when this instinct could combine with others, probably this time the Anglo-Saxons.

It was against these nationalistic policies that Robert Schuman was using his growing influence. He was gradually emerging as the strongest personality in the heterogeneous conglomerate of the MRP which entered the French Legislature as a new party after the liberation. He was fearless in proclaiming his beliefs on European peace, uncompromising in his principles but sufficiently adroit and subtle to survive in the political game. He was attacked by the powerful Communist group and from within the party, with equal vehemence. But it was not long before the Moscow Communists proved themselves Schuman's greatest allies.

Bideault and de Gaulle, with the help of the French Communists, had put forward very specific demands for the incorporation of the Rhineland on the West bank of the Rhine, as well as the Ruhr and the Saar, into France. But to their surprise Mr. Molotov, the Soviet Foreign Minister, who was attending a conference of war-time allies in Paris, violently objected to the French policy and vetoed the destruction of German industrial potential. Obviously, Molotov wanted to preserve a Germany which Moscow could, according to all the indications of the disintegration of Western unity, soon pluck as a ripe but integral plum. It is a curious fact to contemplate today, that it was this disunity amongst war-time allies, a sort of musical chairs being played by each government, with each at a certain time shifting their attitude on the future of Germany, which saved Germany's dismemberment in the West. At one time it had been proposed by Roosevelt. Later it was definitely opposed by Harry Truman, then proposed by Stalin. Earlier Stalin, who was frightened of making his former Western Allies too strong, had at Teheran opposed Churchill who was proposing the breaking-up of Germany by the formation of an Austrian-Bavarian state. Roosevelt at that time seemed sympathetic to breaking Germany up into five different countries but this idea was also turned down by Stalin.

But Robert Schuman was also helped by the Communists in other ways. While on the one hand they refused to support de Gaulle and Bideault on the German question, they also acted in a way which underlined their broader ambitions which had hitherto been ignored by the Western allies. The Marshall Plan had been launched in 1947. Its implementation, however, was practically paralysed by French resistance to German reconstruction, which was envisaged by the plan. But while in February 1948 the Communists were still supporting de Gaulle and Bideault on this question, there came Moscow's *putsch* in Prague. This, coupled with the murder of Czech Foreign Minister Jan Masaryk, put the French Communists in the most awkward position. Even the voluble Thorez found it hard to persuade the gullible French Communists to swallow all this as a liberating move, and practically all other parties were galvanised against Moscow's tactics. Then, a month later, General Sokolovski withdrew as the Soviet member of the Berlin Central Council of Four (Britain, U.S.A., France and USSR). That same month, on March 9th, the "Charter of Frankfurt" had established a sort of German central economic council, later to become Germany's first *de facto* post-war administrative government. As Western reaction to Soviet aggression against the satellites in the East became stronger, particularly with the swallowing-up of Poland and Czechoslovakia, Molotov's attitude of hindrance to French dismemberment of Germany began to change and veer towards an anti-German one. The Western Allies instead now began to look at a restored and viable West Germany as essential to them to counterbalance further Soviet expansion.

In October 1948, Moscow played a dangerous card in the blockade of Berlin, and lost. From October 1948 to March 1949, a formidable air-mobilisation of Western powers defeated the Soviet siege of the city. On March 18th, 1948 Robert Schuman, now Prime Minister of France, advocated in a national radio address the adoption by France of the North Atlantic Defence Treaty, thus indicating a complete reorientation of France towards the West and away from Moscow. By December 1st, 1949, the Defence Council of NATO convened in Paris to work out specific military plans for the defence of the Atlantic Zone. This created considerable difficulty for France as the Franco-Soviet Pact, negotiated by Bideault and de Gaulle and signed on December 10th, 1945, was still in force. When Robert Schuman stood before the deputies to defend NATO, he was bitterly attacked by the Communist group, powerful enough in the Chamber to ensure that Schuman gave assurances to the deputies that Germany should remain disarmed. Less than ten years later, the Western allies, including France, were urging a reluctant Germany to set up the German army, something both Schuman and Adenauer had hoped could be avoided.

As the Soviet menace grew, the unification of a Free Europe, including Germany, began to preoccupy two Frenchmen, Robert Schuman and Jean Monet. Actually, such a plan had been proposed earlier by Adenauer and Arnold, the Christian Democrat representing the new German province of North Rhine-Westphalia. It had also been mooted by De Gasperi. But it was Robert Schuman and Jean Monet who, foreseeing the political barriers to any plan of this kind, began to think that an economic integration could more effectively pave the way for a political cooperation later. Out of these considerations there later emerged the Schuman Plan. It is not minimising the role of Robert Schuman to say that one of the most valuable aspects of his contribution on the arduous way to peace was the fact that he represented France. Adenauer and De Gasperi, both politically and intellectually, over a long period of time and in the face of particular difficulties had achieved singular positions of strength in their own countries, enabling them to shape events, but Schuman held the key to their final success. If at the crucial time he had failed to bring France to the support of eventual European union neither Germany nor Italy would have had a friend at court, in the council of the Allies. Because Schuman sat among the victors, and because of his own political achievements in post-war France, the efforts of Adenauer and De Gasperi were successful.

CHAPTER X

Battle for Europe in Italy

ALCIDE DE GASPERI was the first to establish parliamentary government amongst the defeated Axis powers, after an interregnum first of military government and then gradual emergence of rule by elected representatives.

Before the wider problems of Italy could be resolved, the immediate position (which included Italy's physical boundaries) had to be defined and defended. The tedious and trying negotiations on Trieste lasted several days in London and continued to overshadow Italy's relations with the outside world for some time. The United States Secretary of State, James Byrnes, was opposed to the Yugoslav occupation of Trieste and Venezia Giulia, but the British retained some anti-Italian feeling which prevented them from putting up a strong fight against the Communist front. Vyacheslav Molotov, speaking for Moscow, openly supported the Communist front in Yugoslavia, taunting the West, brushing aside questions of legality and merely stressing the strategic value this occupation had for the Eastern block. From the history of those negotiations, one must conclude that while De Gasperi argued the claims of the Italian population to be part of Italy, the real battle was fought between Moscow and the Western Allies, and Italy could only hope to obtain redress to the extent the West was willing to resist Moscow's westward move.

De Gasperi fought a lone battle. He had several meetings with Molotov in London, in Paris and at other sessions of the Conference, and rightly estimated that the only chance lay in trying to induce Molotov to abandon some of his intransigence. Even postponing a decision of the Allies was some advantage for De Gasperi[1]. A postponement at least left on record a non-recognition of the military occupation by Yugoslav troops of Trieste and its surroundings.

Months later, at a meeting in the Luxembourg Palace in Paris, an agreement was reached whereby Trieste and the adjoining area

[1] Adstans, *De Gasperi Nella Politica Estera Italiana* (Mondadori, Milan.)

were evacuated and placed under the military control of the Western Allies, envisaging an eventual return of Trieste to Italy. This was a great victory, but a victory marred by the sad loss of large areas which had an Italian population and which were sacrificed to Yugoslavia's military coup. Nevertheless, De Gasperi had made a good fight against very great difficulties. Ann O'Hare McCormick commented on the Paris Conference in the *New York Times* that the "agony of the position of De Gasperi was that he had to suffer punishment for the sins committed by another regime, a regime which he had fought all his life", and Dorothy Thompson, writing in the *New York Herald*, said under the title *An open letter to Signor De Gasperi*, "In vain you equate the cause of Italy and that of civilisation; you ask for a peace on principle while your judges are carrying on an autopsy of civilisation. You do not address a conference of peace, but a conference of war. Yes, you Sir have the right to represent yourself as an anti-Fascist and a Democrat, because you did not embrace Mr. Ribbentrop under the swastika, as was done by one who is now sitting as your judge" (Vyacheslav Molotov, who signed the Molotov-Ribbentrop Pact).

Nevertheless, it was a considerable achievement for it later transpired that, several years previously Molotov, had promised Tito all of Venezia Giulia as recompense for his participation in the guerilla action against the Germans.[1]

By February 10th, 1947 the Peace Treaty had been signed at the Quay d'Orsay in Paris, and again De Gasperi fought a tenacious fight. Meli Lupi di Soragna, the Italian Ambassador, was empowered to sign the Treaty subject to its ratification by the Italian parliament. Britain immediately protested and demanded unconditional signature. On February 8th, De Gasperi made a declaration before the Italian parliament, rejecting the British protest but acknowledging that he was fully aware of the blatant contradiction between the terms of the peace treaty now offered and the Atlantic Charter, which prescribed that no exchange of territorial possessions involving population would be valid without the consent of the population directly involved.

De Gasperi refused to budge under British pressure. He stated that the situation embodied the basic principle that Italy could only act under a democratic government if its own elected representatives were accepted as sovereign. If the Italian government could act, as the British had urged, without parliamentary ratification, it would be as in Mussolini's day, when parliament could not control the actions of the executive. He instructed his Foreign

[1] Ibid., page 64.

Minister Sforza to hand the British Ambassador a note to this effect. His argument could not be refuted by Britain and the Treaty was signed in Paris on February 10th by Meli Lupi di Soragna at a "cold and brief ceremony".[1]

On March 20th, 1948 Allied occupation of Trieste ended, amid Soviet protests, and the city, including the Free Zone, was turned over to Italy, but with the loss of Gorizia, Pola and other Italian areas.

Under Soviet pressure, the terms of the Treaty were extremely harsh. The Italian navy was to be divided between Soviet Russia, Britain, the United States and France. Large reparations were to be made by Italy to all the Allies. Considerable diplomatic and economic restrictions were imposed on foreign relations. Undaunted, De Gasperi relied on the realities of politics and the ultimate good sense of the Western Allies, especially in the face of the mounting Communist danger to the West both from Moscow and in Italy itself. He did not miscalculate.

No sooner was the Treaty signed to appease Moscow than the Western Allies decided to forego their share of war loot. Under the leadership of the United States, they did not demand the surrender of the specified naval units given them by the Treaty, although Soviet Russia took her share. The United States not only cancelled reparations, but undertook to pay for the American army stationed in Italy to bolster Italy's balance of payments, and commercial credits were extended. Great Britain and France followed suit. Soviet Russia, on the other hand, not only demanded the payment of the hundred million dollars indemnity fixed by the Treaty, but refused to accept the $177,000,000 counterclaim for confiscated Italian properties in Russia and in the satellite states, setting an arbitrary value on the Italian assets of eleven million dollars only. This brought Italian payments in kind and in cash to a total of $267,000,000, only possible on loans from the Western Allies.

The seriousness of the Italian economic situation is illustrated by an incident mentioned by Paolo Canali. On November 11th, 1946, De Gasperi learned that there were exactly two weeks' supply of grain left in Italy, based on the minimum ration of 300 grams per day per person. No new shipments were expected and he did not know where to turn, having exhausted all approaches and warned the Western Allies and their military commanders in Italy. Canali recalls that De Gasperi then did a most unorthodox thing in politics. He picked up the telephone and made a trans-Atlantic call to Fiorello La Guardia, former Mayor of New York and at that

[1] Ibid, page 98.

time Director of UNRRA. He told La Guardia that in two weeks Italy would literally be faced with starvation, and begged him to take extraordinary measures. It worked. Within hours ships loaded with grain for American troops in Germany were diverted to Italy; others were loaded and another crisis had been averted.

The end of 1946 saw De Gasperi fighting to establish some semblance of ordinary administration in his own country, and at the same time struggling for Italian national rehabilitation against formidable odds at the Conference in the Luxemburg Palace which was drawing up the Peace Treaty. During my first meeting with him at the Palazzo Chigi, he told me: "Italy looks to the wealthy countries of the New World to help her regain a state of free democracy and to maintain it against the new threat of totalitarianism".

Shortly before the signing of the Peace Treaty, De Gasperi received an invitation from Henry Luce, then publisher of *Time–Life–Fortune*, to take part in a conference to which he was inviting leading men from various countries to discuss the subject, "What does the World expect of the U.S.A.?" Recalling the glacial reception he had received in London in 1945, De Gasperi at first hesitated. Also, he was anxious lest the United States Government should feel it improper for the Head of the Italian Government to make the first visit to the United States under private auspices. When Luce's representative visited him at the Viminale, De Gasperi spoke quite frankly of his reservations and apparently, on his return to Washington, Secretary of State Byrnes was taken into confidence. Almost immediately Byrnes extended an official invitation to Alcide De Gasperi, as Prime Minister of Italy, to visit Washington, and he was able to accept the invitation of Henry Luce. It was an opportunity De Gasperi had been waiting for, as he realised that at that critical stage it was to the United States he would have to look for help, when the extreme economic hardships of his people were adversely affecting the chances of establishing a democratic structure on the ruins of post-war Italy.

The first trip to North America proved to be an important turning point. In meetings with Byrnes and his successor, General Marshall, with President Truman and with American industrialists and bankers, De Gasperi was able for the first time to give a detailed picture of the Italian situation and, just as important, to outline his concrete plans for rebuilding a free government. The immediate need was economic, and on that point he received the most sympathetic understanding.

The generosity of the United States, both governmental and public, in the re-building of Europe in post-war years, will probably go down in history as unique. The United States has been exposed to much criticism for its political errors. The United States themselves had to pay so dearly with the lives of their own men, paying for having misjudged Joseph Stalin's ambitions at Teheran, Yalta, Casablanca and Potsdam. She was largely paying for Franklin Roosevelt's illusions of dealing with an uncle Joe. But when all these political errors were recounted, one should never lose sight of the tremendous generosity of the United States, expressed in the Marshall Plan and also in the treatment of their former enemies like Italy, Germany and Japan on questions of reparations and questions of post-war financing and industrial assistance.

Not only was De Gasperi able on the occasion of a later trip to the United States to obtain a one hundred million dollar loan, and generous compensations to Italy for supplies purchased from the Italians by the United States military establishment in Italy. Washington also cancelled claims against properties of Italians in the United States, which had been sequestrated as an alien enemy asset.

If there was one weakness in the generosity of the United States, it was the fact that the U.S. government over-estimated the political strength, as well as political durability, of material aid. They overestimated the ability of their money to buy themselves out of political difficulties. Problems had historical roots, involved national emotions and, above all, had their origin in individual people, not in collective concepts like "state" and "government". Since most benefits of the type De Gasperi obtained merely warded off worse disasters to come, they were largely preventive. But such benefits seldom, if ever, evoke recognition in the average citizen. It is hard for him to imagine something which had not happened and therefore it hardly ever induces gratitude. The citizen, like any other individual usually counts amongst his blessings only that which has been added, not what has not been lost. It is strange that after years of experience in Latin America, where Americans themselves coined a somewhat cynical phrase, "You can buy them, but they won't stay bought", the United States, with the undaunted optimism of the New World, harboured hopes of a "firm purchase of friendship" in the Old World.

Generous United States material help, distributed by well-meaning but singularly insular United States officials, was aided and abetted by equally unsophisticated U.S. Information officials. Much of its effect, politically, was lost. A loaf of bread handed to a starving Europe with one hand and a U.S. propaganda pamphlet showing the "beauties of democracy" with the other, depicting the U.S. citizen with butter and jam, rolling in wealth, easily evoked jealousy rather than admiration.

During this first important visit of De Gasperi to the United States I had the good fortune, with the help of my friend Paolo Canali, who was accompanying De Gasperi as his secretary, to have another interview with De Gasperi while the latter was in Cleveland. His own words expressed the gist of his hopes. When I spoke to him of his trip years later, he would refer to it as having been the turning point in giving Italy, at a desperate moment, the contacts and the help on which she could continue to build. Neither De Gasperi nor Canali ever lacked appreciation for material aid and the warmth and understanding of their own reception in the States, even when policy differences arose between Washington and Rome on international issues.

One of the remarkable things which impressed me in my conversations with De Gasperi in those difficult years was the fact that while he seemed to be so completely preoccupied with the immediate critical problems of the Italian people, this never obscured his wider horizons. He constantly kept before him a clear vision of a larger Europe, unified and strengthened, making its contribution to a world order of peace and justice. In this he had a close collaborator, tried friend and competent assistant in the person of Count Sforza, his Foreign Minister for many years. Like so many of the great statesmen of post-war Europe, Count Sforza had had his difficulties with the Allies, and in the early days was excluded from the Italian government because the British did not consider him sufficiently malleable. It was De Gasperi who finally insisted on giving Sforza the post of Foreign Minister in his own government, when no allied veto remained.

Maria Romana Catti De Gasperi, his eldest daughter, travelled with him on various occasions as his private secretary and was probably the person closest to him. In her biography of her father[1] she points to what might be considered almost a paradox: De Gasperi from his earliest days had been involved in politics, fighting for the rights of his people. Still, as Maria Romana says, he was never a fiery nationalist. "He did not believe according to any seventeenth century formulae, that God has marked certain demarcation lines on our globe dividing the human creatures along certain borders which they would have to defend with their lives. Already while he was still at school Italian civilization had fascinated him as he was discovering in his reading of the classics the reasons for national pride. But already he was a citizen of Europe", Maria Romana wrote. De Gasperi was involved in hard and difficult negotiations on "geographical frontiers" when he was defending Italy's claim to

[1] *De Gasperi Uomo Solo,* Maria Romana Catti De Gasperi (Mondadori, Milan).

the Upper-Adige (South Tirol), the different demarcation lines proposed for Venezia Giulia, and again in his opposition to the French claims on territory along the Piedmont border.

Maria Romana explains how, in the battle for the Italians of Venezia Giulia, he was fighting for people who were forced to abandon their homes and their land. It was never *against* the neighbouring country that he would feel any sense of rivalry, she wrote, but only sympathy for suffering individuals and particularly those suffering injustice.

De Gasperi saw no future, either for Italy or any other country in Europe, except in unison and cooperation, and for this reason he became not only the instigator, but also the strongest protagonist of a European Federation. For him the battle for Europe began practically at the same time as his battle for a freely constituted democratic Italy. Even before the Peace Treaty had been ratified by the Italian Legislature, on September 15th, 1947, De Gasperi was actively engaged in promoting the idea of cooperation with the establishment of NATO, working towards a pact of European Defence, the C.E.D., and at the same time looking to the O.E.E.C. (Organisation of European Economic Cooperation) as a basis on which to develop his country's policies. When the E.R.P., the so called Marshall Plan (European Rehabilitation Programme) was first discussed, De Gasperi exchanged ideas with Truman. They both saw the reciprocal dependence "on which your well-being depends as much as our own", as the underlying purpose of the plan. It was largely due to De Gasperi's efforts in Paris that dangerous delays in the implementation of the Marshall Plan were shortened before French obstructions would have made all help for Europe arrive too late.

When De Gasperi addressed the First European Parliament on May 5th, 1949, in the Palace of Europe in Strasbourg, it was generally recognised that he had indicated the foundations on which post-war peace could be built. Above all he indicated the absolute necessity for a joint ideal of unity, in place of the dangerous spirit of nationalism which had caused so much evil, and acknowledged that, in losing the war, Italy had lost many of her illusions.

In order that De Gasperi could play his full role in the European efforts at finding a way to a more lasting peace, he had to establish himself on the domestic front. After several failures of the others to agree on a constructive policy, De Gasperi became Prime Minister on December 10th, 1945, presiding over a cabinet consisting of all the parties represented in the C.L.N., including the Communists. Admiral Stone, in the name of the Allies, confirmed their civil jurisdiction over "all Italian territories from (the island of) Pantelleria to the Brenner (Pass) with the exception of Udine, to remain under direct authority of the occupying forces, the same as Venezia Giulia".

When the first elections took place on June 2nd, 1946 to the Constituent Assembly, it was to everybody's surprise, except the Christian Democrats themselves, that they elected 207 representatives, as against 115 to the Socialists who were the next largest party. The Communists elected 104 members while the Liberals, once the leading party, only obtained 41 representatives out of a combination and coalition of Liberals including such rivals as Orlando, Nitti and Bonomi. The elections to the Constituent Assembly were held at the same time as a plebiscite was also voted upon regarding the future form of government, Monarchist or Republican. The Republicans obtained a majority.

It was De Gasperi who had to deal with King Umberto II and arrange for the transition from Monarchy to Republic, with Enrico de Nicola becoming Head of State as President. De Gasperi naturally had to deal with a number of domestic problems all the way from the immediate supply of food to more basic and permanent problems like social programmes and property rights, including land reform.

In the natural revulsion to many of the inhuman practices of Fascism and particularly Nazism, it is too easily forgotten or might have been completely overlooked that both these regimes were extremely advanced in some of their social legislation, compared with the Liberal-Democratic regimes they succeeded.

For this reason De Gasperi had foreseen in the immediate postwar situation, with the emergence of the two great Marxist forces, Socialist and Communist, the absolute need to contest their social programmes with something which was more than just another social programme with a Christian label. De Gasperi was convinced that the exponents of Liberal Democracy could not challenge the Marxists. The Liberals were without any ideology which, based on the moderating counsels of Christian social unity and social justice, and rooted in a brotherhood of man, was unthinkable if divorced from the fatherhood of God.

As successor to the Fascists, De Gasperi had to establish a government over a people who had suffered under Mussolini but had also benefited from some of his social measures. As well as their politically criminal activities, Hitler and Mussolini had also carried through very extensive modes of material protection of the worker. This was in relation both to his employer and to matters of health insurance, sanitary working conditions, pensions and even opportunities for leisure (*Kraft durch Freude*). However, there was nothing voluntary about it, as the worker no longer had the right to elect his own union representative, nor even select a union. Everything was organised for him by the central government on the lines of extreme paternalism. The workers now received more and more extensive benefits and greater security of employment and even increased wages (though this was usually counteracted by inflation). This appeared to the worker far more concrete a benefit than just the right to free elections.

As European General Manager for the United Press, I was an employer in those years in both Italy and Germany. This meant I was constantly involved with the Nazi newspaper council, *Presse-kammer*, in Germany and the *Fascio della Stampa*, the Italian counterpart, with regard to our employees in those countries. With my headquarters in London, it was my constant duty on frequent visits to supervise the bureaux in those countries under dictatorship.

Hence from personal experience I had noted the extent to which in contracts of employment, social and medical insurance, pension plans and grievances against management, the employees were far better protected than their counterparts in the free countries which were under what was more or less liberal Capitalism. In exchange they traded in their political freedom.

De Gasperi was made particularly aware of what he had to face in the social legislation of Mussolini, whose Fascist paternalism, no less than that of the Communists, was not always aimed at the welfare of the worker as much as it was at undermining or destroying private initiative. This, incidentally, often led to certain misunderstandings on the part of the generous United States' representatives. They saw both De Gasperi and Adenauer developing and promulgating certain social legislation which, according to American free capitalist standards, was considered extravagant and hence annoying to those who at that time were financing the deficits of the newly formed democratic regimes.

Even from my own personal observations, the situation of the domestic development of Italy was, I could see, one requiring great political skill. Both Adenauer and De Gasperi possessed considerable diplomatic skill for international relations as well as the gift of being good domestic politicians. This ability was largely responsible for keeping them both in power, and that was the first prerequisite for all their activities that were intended to bring about the unification of Europe and international peace.

CHAPTER XI

Challenge from the East

IN a dispatch to the United Press from Frankfurt in June 1946 I pointed out that a year after occupation there was as yet no sign or even semblance of a return to productive work on the part of the population of Germany. I wrote then: "There will be none, officials told me, until the powers have decided what activities are permitted. In the meantime 70,000,000 people are more or less soup-kitchen wards of the Americans".[1]

The Allies were interested in "re-education" of the Germans for political stabilisation, but the greatest drawback in re-education at that time was lack of news from outside Germany. As I wrote in another report "The newspapers are pitifully inadequate, scarce and small. The German ignorance about conditions abroad is abysmal. Hitler had them hermetically sealed off, but he gave them information—even if false information. We have also sealed them off, but have given them no substitute".

"American and British newspapers and periodicals are completely barred. There is no more contact with the outside world than in Hitler's day, except they can listen to the Moscow Radio without being shot for it. The Berlin Sender, the powerful radio station run by the Soviets, is reputed to have the biggest listening audience in the Western Zone, and there they do not hear 'You are guilty!', but they hear a lot about how well-off the Germans are in the Russian Zone, with news items of distress in the Western Zone."

"Few young men take an active interest in politics. All societies have been suppressed because in the Third Reich most of them were '*gleichgeschaltet*', which means nazified. The only groups that have kept themselves clear of Nazi influence have been the Protestant Church Organisation of the Confessional Movement, and they were mostly driven underground by Hitler and hence led a semi-catacomb existence with only handfuls of members among the

[1] *Montreal Star*, June 17th, 1946, page 1.

young, and the Catholic parish organisations which right up to the end the Nazis did not dare to touch, only harass."

Nowhere in those days did I find such clear, all-encompassing, yet unbiased vision, as, during a private audience with Pope Pius XII, when we discussed at length the vexed question of public information. During my Rome visit, a personal experience illustrated the difficulty of ordinary everyday contact. I had occasion to have various conversations with Father Robert Leiber, S.J., and after my private audience he came to see me at my hotel. He had a letter from the Pope and asked if I would take this to Frankfurt and hand it to the Apostolic Delegate to Germany, who was at that time, Father Zeiger, S.J. I was surprised that I should be asked to carry such a letter, especially after I had told him that I would first be going to Paris and would not be in Frankfurt much before ten days to a fortnight.

Father Leiber explained that it would still be of great assistance to him to have this important dispatch taken to the Apostolic Delegation. "Do you realise that we are not permitted to communicate with our own Delegate in Germany? The Holy See is kept completely *incommunicado*, except where they can utilise 'black' facilities of the kind I am now asking you to offer us".

I put the large envelope with some letters into my pocket and a fortnight later, when I was in Frankfurt, drove across the Main River to the villa where Father Zeiger was living. He was deeply grateful to this improvised "papal-courier" and while I naturally did not ask what the content of the letter was, I was told that this was most important and could help a great deal in his very difficult work. He went on to explain that even the *Osservatore Romano* was banned in the general policy of not "fraternising" with the German people, and he described the dangerous situation. Every book could be imported from the Soviet Zone and every facility was being offered the Communist agitators as allies. In the meantime every communication with the West was being cut off by the Western authorities themselves, because they still obeyed regulations which apparently the Roosevelt regime had laid down as part of the Morgenthau Plan. The rest of the Plan had been ditched, but those minor regulations were being applied rigidly, unimaginatively and most dangerously.

As I speak Russian, I had an opportunity during this visit to Germany to talk at official dinners with Soviet military personnel who, perhaps animated by the hospitality, or because they were able to speak to me in their own language, became somewhat loquacious. They would ridicule our efforts at "re-educating" the Germans and sarcastically analysed their own propaganda successes. "In large measure", one Soviet Colonel said, "the stupidity of your people is leaving the whole field to us!" He boasted quite openly that it would not be long before they would be able to "pluck the ripe plum" of West Germany. In fact other vital forces were already stirring in the political, intellectual and spiritual life of Germany, but I could not blame the Soviet Colonel for not noticing them. It was a dangerous time and the danger was largely of our own making.

At the time Konrad Adenauer was organising his party, I had an interesting conversation with the leader of the Bavarian branch of his Christian Democratic Union, Dr. Joseph Müller. The latter was more than a political leader, having a most interesting background of resistance and underground activity during the war. "Neither Germany nor Europe can ever be reconstructed on the old lines as national states, nor can such an attempt spell anything but the end of our Western civilisation", he told me.

As one of the most active leaders in the German underground, who had also been a key member of the German military intelligence, Dr. Müller had managed to get abroad on many occasions, especially to Rome. There he got in touch with emissaries of the Allies and had military information transmitted to London, Brussels and Paris. I asked him point-blank how he, as a German, felt about communicating with the enemies of his country during the war, and carrying on negotiations with American and British diplomats.

"When you feel a criminal has taken possession of your home and imprisoned your family, then you ask your neighbours to help you to oust him, should you be lucky enough to establish contact with these neighbours while the other members of the family are gagged, tied and under the vigilance of that armed thug", was the gist of his reply.

I quoted him on the subject of the new party formation on which he was working with Konrad Adenauer,[1] "Our union is a group of kindred spirits and the only choice we have left, namely, whether to preserve a system of individual liberty which alone can be based on the Christian concept of man, or else accept the alternative of degradation and disappointment—the materialist solution of a collective state of totalitarianism. Our political union by no means is a Catholic party, but a complete partnership of Protestants and Catholics growing out of the common resistance movement against Nazi collectivism. While I am a Catholic, the Vice-President of the Bavarian group is a Protestant, and while Bavaria is predominantly Catholic, similar support is given us by Protestant regions."

[1] *Montreal Star*, June 18, 1946, page 1.

Müller then described how he, with his Chief of Military Intelligence, the late Admiral Canaris, General Oster and others, conspired to oust Hitler. The attempt on Hitler's life on July 20th, 1944 led to the execution of his co-conspirators and a savage, widespread blood purge. He was put in a concentration camp and only saved from execution by the timely arrival of Allied troops. His wife and his secretary had also been in a concentration camp and he recounted the tortures and indignities to which they were all subjected.

He felt that, "one of the greatest mistakes of the Western World is to suppose that they can mould or order the political future of Germany". Having combatted totalitarian collectivism in Germany, as imposed by Hitler, long before the arrival of the now victorious allies, and having faced the hangman's noose as a traitor to the Nazi regime during the war against Hitler, Müller felt entitled to speak as an experienced political veteran. There really did exist a political vacuum, he insisted, in which 70 million disillusioned and destitute Germans, were an (as yet) undefined mass but who had a potential political force which could be easily harnessed. Either they would follow advocates of a parliamentary democracy like Adenauer and the other determined foes of both brands of totalitarianism (Hitler's brown variety or Stalin's red one) or else they would succumb to the blandishments of freedom's enemies who were working freely in the occupied zone.

Müller pointed out that while much depended on the efforts of his group, the credibility of their campaign assurances in turn depended largely on conditions which were entirely in the hands of the military occupation forces.

"To-day you (the Western allies) can decide Germany's future. But failing that, Germany might decide your future by joining the even larger unit, namely, the Soviet orbit", Müller warned in the interview.

The odds which the German advocates of parliamentary democracy were facing was illustrated to me later in the day. After an early morning interview with Müller in Munich I had driven to Nürnberg to attend the "war-criminals" trial. While exchanging a few words with a friend on Justice Jackson's U.S. staff in the hotel, which had been requisitioned for the U.S. judicial commission, the telephone rang. It was Dr. Müller, to whom I had mentioned where I would be in the afternoon, should he be in Nürnberg, which was within his Franconian constituency in which he was campaigning. Thinking that my friend would be interested in meeting this outstanding enemy of Hitler I suggested Müller come up to the room. "But he is a German, we can't fraternise with him" was the horrified reaction of my friend. So I left to meet Müller and found him patiently waiting on the curb outside with two GI's, who were obviously Californian Japanese (Nisei) barring the way for this freedom fighter, barred from contact with the new "Herrenvolk". It reminded me of my Soviet table-companion of a few days ago, chuckling over Western ineptness in winning the fruits of their military victory.

It was men like these who had to solve the practical problem, not only for themselves, but also, as Müller pointed out, for the free world.

Earlier that year, on March 5th at Fulton, Missouri, Winston Churchill had delivered his famous "iron-curtain" address calling for an Anglo-American understanding to protect themselves against the Soviet Union. A few days later, the then American Secretary of the Navy, James Forrestal, met Churchill in London and made an entry into his diary about the hour-and-a-quarter spent together. Forrestal noted: "He (Churchill) was very gloomy about coming to any accommodation with Russia unless it became clear to the Russians that they would be met with force if they continued with their expansion."

Forrestal then noted that Churchill agreed with his analysis that the Western allies were not merely dealing with today's Soviet Russia but "with the expanding Russia under Peter the Great, plus the additional force of their (political) religion".[1]

Significant evidence of the rising danger of Soviet military intervention to back their political ambitions in Western Europe is supplied by Forrestal in his entry for May 3rd, 1946: "The Secretary of War called me this evening to say that a message had come from McNarney (General Joseph T. McNarney, Commander of the United States Forces in Europe), asking for permission from the War Department to dispatch troops from the American area in Germany to France, should there be an attempted overturn of the government by the Communist wing, following the voting on the proposed new French constitution on Sunday. . . Thorez, head of the French Communist Party, is in favour of a coup d'état".[2]

Fears of the Germans like Müller and Adenauer that Europe was in danger of being lost to the West were thus not unfounded, and were shared by the men in the highest posts of Allied responsibility.

It was against this atmosphere that Konrad Adenauer had to build from scratch a political movement which was strong enough not only numerically, but also in the fervour of their convictions, to fill the political vacuum so as to (using Joseph Müller's phrase) "lead a dazed mass of 70 million Germans".

[1] *The Forrestal Diaries*, ed. by Walter Millis (Viking Press).
[2] Ibid.

Against this background, Adenauer's fundamental need was to rebuild democracy, and for that he first had to create a non-existent party. The old *Zentrum* (Catholic Party) having been resuscitated by Allied decree, merely brought some surviving political figures into the advisory bodies set up by the Allies. The actual moribund condition of that former political expression, the Zentrum, became apparent only too soon. Like De Gasperi's *Popolari* who, with a few exceptions, had voted for the law which bestowed legal dictatorial power upon Mussolini, the *Zentrum* had also committed political suicide, under the direction of its chairman, Monsignor Kaas, by voting for Hitler's "Empowering Laws". This double political suicide of the so-called Catholic parties of Germany and Italy seemed to be ignored by the political advisors of Allied military government.

The *Zentrum* was born during the bitter battles for religious rights, the *Kulturkampf*, in the days of Bismarck and actually belonged to the nineteenth century. As Adenauer conceived it, that was too narrow an issue for the political future of Germany. As mentioned in his memoirs, the creation of a new political party at first sight seemed hopeless. His almost spontaneous response to the idea of a Christian union of Catholics and Protestants was to describe it as a "political miracle". If we compare the situation of Adenauer and that of De Gasperi at that time, we must remember that Adenauer faced the task of creating an entirely new party. De Gasperi, in organising the Christian Democrats, was able to mobilise support from at least some former members of the *Popolari*, but in spite of that he faced an extremely difficult assignment.

But in Adenauer's case, far from being supported, he ran into violent opposition from many of his old party friends. They had rallied to the resurrected party skeleton of former days and saw in the Christian Democrats of Adenauer not only rivals, but impostors even. There was no doubt that there was rivalry, but once genuine elections were permitted, the majority of former *Zentrum* voters rallied to the Christian Democrats and the old *Zentrum* was literally voted out of existence, and has since disappeared.

That the idea of a Christian Democratic party was not new to Konrad Adenauer can be seen from a statement he made as far back as 1922. He had been chosen that year to preside at the large national annual rally of Catholics in Germany, known as the *Katholikentag*. It was held in Munich. On that occasion Adenauer somewhat startled the gathering by saying:

"In our battle to assert Christian principles in public life we must seek allies among the non-Catholics and weaken as far as possible any opposition from amongst those whom we cannot win to our cause. Maybe, or even truly, we have kept ourselves too distant from the non-Catholics. In this way we have not furthered our common Christian ideals. As much as it is possible, we must go hand in hand with those in the Evangelical camp who have the same goals to achieve, and we must support and sustain each other".

In his autobiography Adenauer recalls how, because of the Nazi terror, he had been unable to devote himself to the activities in public life to which he was wholeheartedly dedicated. "I had lost my wife as a result of her imprisonment, which caused her fatal illness. I had experienced the results of the war. Three of my sons were at the front, causing me daily anxiety. One of them was seriously wounded", he wrote, and went on to describe how he had seen "where an atheistic dictatorship can lead man".

He had heard of the extermination of the Jews and the cruelty perpetrated by Germans upon Germans; he had seen his whole people collapse into chaos. Now he saw a new threat: the very tangible danger of a dictatorship of the Communist variety. He mentions how the certainty gradually took root and grew in him and in others, that only on the foundation of Christian ethics could a practical basis be found for the task of reformation and reconstruction.

Almost spontaneously, he notes, groups sharing these ideas were being formed throughout the land. The most important presupposition was that their members would be democrats who were prepared to give expression to their political convictions and direction to their political activities on the basis of Christian principles. The basic concept, that the dignity of the human person transcends all governmental power, derives directly from the very nature of Western Christianity, he wrote.

Golo Mann in his book on Germany[1] gives expression to the sophisticated Western opposition to Adenauer's thesis. The prevalence of those who deny fundamental principles and ideological realities has been a weakening factor to the West when it faced the modern barbarism of totalitarian power.

"What then was National Socialism? It was an historically unique phenomenon, dependent on an individual and on a moment, a phenomenon which can never reappear in the same form. It was a state of intoxication produced by a gang of intoxicated experts, kept up for a few years. It was a machine for the manufacture of power, for the safeguarding of power and for the extention of power. The machine was located in Germany and therefore used to

[1] *The History of Germany since 1789* (Chatto & Windus, London; Frederick Praeger, New York), page 446.

fuel German energies, German interests, passions and ideas. We want power—this cry of the year 1932 was the essence of the new message. Power meant organisation, indoctrination and the authority to give orders; it meant the suppression of all independent life, of anything capable of resistance. In that sense it was essentially a negative element. The power of National Socialism over Germany thus only became complete when the Reich was close to collapse, when its army had already been defeated. The determination to have power was considerable; the doctrine was not. Who can say today what the Nazis thought?"

Mann's definition explains in a way why the bourgeoisie of Germany, as well as of Great Britain and the United States, were unable for so long to draw the essential parallel between Nazism, Fascism and Communism, which were all three political expressions of a basic refusal to accept the Christian definition of the dignity and hence rights of the individual. Born of the Christian concept, strongly furthered by Christian Protestant inspiration, liberalism had espoused the rights of man against the disregard of these rights in the older feudal and post-feudal hierarchical societies of the Western world. But as liberalism lost its religious content, though still surviving strongly in the nineteenth century amongst liberals like William Gladstone, the political motivation also altered. Turning instead to the positivism or relativism of men like Havelock Ellis, Chief Justice Hughes, H. G. Wells, Bertrand Russell, to name but a few in the Anglo-Saxon world, and to the men who also inspired the literati of France, Italy and Germany at the turn of the century, not least amongst them Thomas, the father, and Heinrich the uncle of Golo Mann, we suddenly see a large and essential element of Western brilliance maintaining a secularised liberalism bereft of spiritual content.

No one who had closely studied the thoughts that inspired Father Delp, Pastor Bonhoeffer (both of whom died in concentration camps), Cardinal Faulhaber and Pastor Niemoeller and many others in their opposition to Nazism, and read the attacks upon them by Alfred Rosenberg and lesser prophets of Nazi ideology, would ask the question, "Who can say what the Nazis thought?" A closer study of the victims of Mussolini, such as De Gasperi, or the many men Communism has destroyed, could readily answer such a question.

Thus the real political battles which shaped the twentieth century, saw the rise first of urbane liberal materialism, and its natural corollary, atheism (anti-religious), which soon developed into extremism. Western extremism, expressed politically in Communism, Fascism and Nazism, was first ignored and later misunderstood by the rulers of the West. The mandarins in their pleasant intellectual ivory towers, whether on the Thames, the Seine, the Tiber or the Spree were so civilised that they did not believe "religious wars" could happen in the twentieth century. Such vulgarity could in any case never win.

One only has to read the memoirs of Harold Nicolson (excellently edited by his son Nigel), the biographies of Chip Kenan, of Anthony Eden or even Lord Beaverbrook and others who understood and defended their "establishments", to realise how shallow, how callow and insensitive to the fundamental issues of ideology these men had become.

It certainly would not be true to say that they were callow and insensate by nature. They deeply felt and strongly reacted to every nicety in other fields. But they suddenly found themselves faced with the necessity of coping with primordial, or what they would call "primitive", forces that they had long considered abolished with the growth of literacy, sanitation and modern technology. They had conveniently relegated profound spiritual conviction to the realm of "religious prejudices", if not to "regrettable superstition".

Because of their anti-Catholic convictions the prevalent attitude of Western statesmen tended to support such political figures in France, Italy and Germany, as the Socialists and anti-clerical Liberals. Ideas about the Church in general and the men of Christian Democrat political expression, Adenauer, Schuman and De Gasperi in particular, were well formulated by Gabriel A. Almond of Yale University when he wrote in November, 1948, in the *Journal of Politics*: "The rise of Fascist movements during the inter-war period (1918–39) found the majority of the Catholic populations of Western Europe quite susceptible to authoritarian appeals". That Hitler had to transfer from Catholic Bavaria to Berlin, which was only nominally Protestant and where religious life had eroded, because he found insufficient echoes in the population who were listening to the courageous words of Cardinal Faulhaber, and that one voice raised, together with others of course, in Berlin was that of the Cardinal Archbishop of Berlin Count Preysing, echoed by the Cardinal Archbishop Count von Galen in the Rhineland's capital Cologne, seems to have escaped Almond.

Conviction to an agnostic West smacked too much of latent authoritarianism. In those places where conviction accepts religious authority they saw but minions of mediaeval church power. Actually Adenauer and De Gasperi had frequent disagreements with churchmen, when these overstepped their authority on faith and morals and tried unduly to influence politics. In fact Maria

Romana Catti De Gasperi in her book (*De Gasperi Uomo Solo*) devotes quite a few pages to this subject of differences on political methods in Italy between her father and Pius XII.

Here the closing paragraph in the book *Philby—The Spy who Betrayed a Generation*[1] is significant: "But the most important lesson (from Philby's betrayal) is that democracy cannot be defended by people who are themselves politically illiterate and naive. Philby, Burgess and MacLean all survived, essentially, because they passed so much of their careers amongst people who shared, in varying degrees, the comfortable assumption that it was permissible to ignore ideologies which have altered the whole aspect of the twentieth century. 'All the isms and the Wasms', said the foreign office spokesman with magnificent flippancy when the Nazi-Soviet pact was announced. But he was wrong: this remains a century in which people are moved by isms. Philby and his friends have done enough to teach us the lesson. Only if we fail to understand it do they win".

This passage echoes Churchill's reference, as recorded in the *Forrestal Diaries*,[2] to the men in his entourage who had to be condemned for the betrayal of their country's secrets to the Soviets, and who were convinced that they were following a new code of morality.

Adenauer was profoundly conscious of the fact that there had been a sort of religious prudery (dictated by liberal ideas of tolerance and a conviction that a person's beliefs are a private affair) which had given pre-war Europe leaders in the free countries who were more baffled than effective in dealing with Stalin, Hitler and Mussolini. There was a conviction abroad that one should neither inquire into nor probe nor take into account what a man believed, lest one became guilty of religious prejudice. Yet without considering the personal convictions of Lenin or De Gasperi, Adenauer or Mussolini, de Gaulle or Roosevelt, Hitler or Robert Schuman and many others who shaped history according to their compelling beliefs, no accurate evaluation of the real issues can be made. They were all using political means, economic methods or technological facilities which were more or less available to all men of their times, equally to the just as to the unjust. Hence when we outline the main points of Adenauer's political goals and achievements, we must naturally take into account not merely his physical actions, political manoeuvres and personal character, but also his religious motivations.

The flood of literature which, beginning in the late forties and increasing in the fifties and sixties, examined the roles played by the

[1] *Philby—The Spy who Betrayed a Generation*, Page, Letch and Knightley, (André Deutsch, London).
[2] See page 120.

Catholic and Protestant Churches under Hitler, also probed at fundamentals. Doubtless Adenauer, having lived through these years of persecution and oppression, was much more conscious of these issues than a statesman who had not shared this experience, but only heard of it from a safe distance.

It is interesting to note that in a book published as late as 1968 by Professor J. S. Conway, *The Nazi Persecution of the Churches 1933–45*[1] the author says: "It is a regrettable fact that in almost all the accounts by English-speaking authors of the Nazi era in Germany, only slight attention is paid to the affairs of the churches. So much attention has seen paid, and so much focused, on the military and political events of the years of the Nazi tyranny, that the internal developments, with the exception of the resistance movement and the construction of the notorious concentration camps, have largely been overlooked".

As a matter of fact Adenauer was advised against too rigid an ideological party. It had been suggested, especially by the former liberal-conservative Schlange-Schoeningen, that he organise a grouping of former parties, calling it a coalition, rather than a new political structure. Adenauer's biographer, Paul Weymar, wrote: "Compared with its great rival, the Social Democratic party, which was based on a settled programme and whose organisation was able everywhere to rely on the foundations and traditions of the old (pre-Hitler) parties, the Christian Democratic Union was at a great disadvantage . . ."[2]

At the first rally of Adenauer's political supporters at Bad Godesberg in December 1945, and again at the second meeting held at Hertford in Westphalia in 1946, and at the third and most important of the meetings at Neheim-Huesten in the Westerwald near Koblenz in March, 1946, Adenauer constantly insisted that the planks of the platform for his new party must be primarily anti-materialist and anti-collectivist. It was at the third meeting that the most important consideration in the pending task of reconstruction, whether economic, political or cultural, was clearly defined as the safe-guarding of the rights of the individual. To further assure these rights, Adenauer wanted specific guarantees for the rights of minorities against being steam-rollered by a majority vote. He considered an unqualified rule by majority one of the reasons for the Nazi success and felt that a majority should always be restrained by overriding individual basic rights, constitutionally safeguarded, which no politically expedient combination of party votes could curtail.

[1] *The Nazi Persecution of the Churches 1933–45*, Prof. J. S. Conway (Weidenfield & Nicholson, London).

[2] *Adenauer*, Weymar (André Deutsch, London).

The extent to which individual rights and conscience were a fundamental conviction with Adenauer, is illustrated by an incident of a few year later with his own party executive. When in 1949 a German parliament was first convened, and he met his party executive to map out strategy, the question of party discipline was broached and the introduction of the British system of a party whip to ensure solidarity of party vote was proposed. To everybody's surprise Adenauer categorically opposed this, despite the added power it would have given him. He saw in the exercise of the whip undue pressure exerted on the free conscience of a party member. He argued that solidarity could only be expected to the extent to which there was unanimity, freely arrived at by each individual member, and that the right to dissent was equally important and should be safeguarded. Only the cabinet, he insisted, should speak with one voice, and when Dr. Heinemann, then Minister of the Interior (and later to become President of the Federal Republic in 1969) opposed government policy on German rearmament, he was asked to resign from the Cabinet.

In his memoirs, he defined his belief as follows: "Only the Christian concept ensures law, order, moderation, dignity and freedom to the individual person and thus assures a genuine democracy". This was the keynote of the party programme which was ratified at Neheim-Huesten.

Apart from his preoccupation with the structure of his new party, the C.D.U., Adenauer, as President of the Parliamentary Council, also had the arduous task of hammering out the Basic Law from various opposing views of German political parties. This law in fact was to become the constitution of a new Federal Republic, once the Military Council Committee of the United States (General Lucius Clay), Great Britain (Sir Brian Robertson) and France (General Koenig) completed their work of indicating the extent to which Germans could begin to govern themselves. While Adenauer was working with the Parliamentary Council, the Allied Commission worked on a formulation of the so-called Occupation Statute with which the German Basic Law would then have to be co-ordinated.

On the domestic front the argument was mainly on the decision of Adenauer and his C.D.U. to opt for a loose federation of the *Länder* (provinces), each retaining local controls for an organic autonomy in cultural and in some fiscal matters. The Federal government, once constituted, would be restricted primarily to foreign relations, including foreign trade, foreign affairs and defence. The Socialists opposed the federalist position of the C.D.U. They wanted a centralised government which would only leave residual and limited rights of local administration to the provinces. In the Socialist view, the province's principal task would be to administer the executive decisions of the Federal government.

Another point of friction between the C.D.U. and the Socialists centred on the much fought-over Clause 24 of the Basic Law, according to which the Federal government could surrender sovereignty rights whenever necessary by transferring them to a supra-national body. It was on this clause that Adenauer concentrated his energies as the first step towards a European union. He was looking to the day when the merging of interests with France and other countries could eventually take place by the formation of a common European market. It was one of Adenauer's great disappointments in later years that he was unable to merge his own country's defence plans for European security into a European army, and thus avoid the re-establishment of a national German army which was virtually forced upon him by the Western Allies.

When Adenauer visited Winston Churchill in December 1951, he pleaded with Churchill to participate in a joint European army to allay French fears of being left alone with the Germans. He found ready understanding from Churchill as well as from Eden, who both did their best to promote the European Common Defence Plan, which was unfortunately scuttled later by Mendès-France.

In her book, *La Republique des Contradictions*,[1] Georgette Elgey refers to Adenauer's efforts to extirpate from the minds of the German people any militarist ferment, any aspirations of revenge, for what had been the misfortunes of Germany. She then quotes Maurice Schuman, at that time State Secretary of Foreign Affairs, who recounted that: "During negotiations for a European army, Chancellor Adenauer passed a small piece of paper to Robert Schuman. Reading it, the neck of the recipient grew red, proof that he was moved. The words had been written in French, and yet, when these two were together, the two men spoke German. Adenauer had written: 'Attention, this leads us to the resurrection of a German national army, and we do not want any part in it'. Robert Schuman, who collected autographs, told me when he showed it to me: 'I guard it preciously. You can imagine the importance that a thing like this has, addressed by him to me' ". During a meeting of the C.E.D. Maurice Schuman recalls, according to Georgette Elgey: "In the course of a dinner with Jean Monet, Herbert Blankenhorn and myself, Adenauer told us: 'It would be a catastrophe for the world and for Germany should there ever again be German soldiers' ". Elgey speaks of the fear Adenauer had that

[1] *La Republique des Contradictions*, Georgette Elgey (Fayard, Paris).

the existence of a national army might some day be a strong temptation to reconquer territories lost in the East, and thus risk a third world war. "This fear was always present in the mind of the Chancellor. Rhinelander by origin, and a fervent Catholic, he considered Protestant Prussia with distress, Berlin as a 'pagan city' ". Adenauer was not alone in his efforts "to do everything and by all means" in order to avoid the creation of a German army.

She recounts seeing General Ely's notes, which he made as Chief of Staff of the French Army, in which Ely records discussions with the German General Heusinger and General Speidel. Ely was propounding the French idea of a united "Europe of Fatherlands", each with their own army instead of a unified European army, which idea de Gaulle in particular fought most bitterly. If one suppressed the French army one suppressed France, Ely pointed out to the German generals, as he urged the necessity of "preserving a national ideal". To this Heusinger is recorded as having retorted: "I do not believe anything of that". To him it was essential in order to gain German enthusiasm, to give his people a new ideal instead of reviving the old one: nationalism. This new ideal Heusinger is reported as having told Ely was "no more Germany, no more flag, no more territory. Only Europe can be an ideal for the Germans".

While working on the establishment of orderly political life in Germany by the creation of his own strong political party, Adenauer was also preoccupied with negotiations with the Military Control Commission on whom all political life in Germany basically depended. No headway seemed to be possible for a long time because the French representative insisted on territorial control over the Saar and economic rights in the Ruhr, while the British continued dismantling German industries, so creating more unemployment, and doing everything possible to further the political fortunes of the Socialists in Germany. The United States, growing impatient, were urging quick rehabilitation of the German economy for the greater effectiveness of the newly announced Marshall Plan. As the Allies seemed to be at loggerheads, Adenauer decided to take matters into his own hands, and in order to break the deadlock he decided to bring the matter to the attention of a world public. He accepted an invitation from the President of the Swiss section of the Interparliamentary Union, Dr. de Senarclens, to deliver an address on March 22, 1949 in Berlin. Adenauer's speech had the effect of a bombshell, for he used this platform to deliver a startling list of particulars regarding the German situation and its dangers to the Western world.

First he sketched the world situation as he saw it, dominated by two formidable power centres; on the one hand the members of the

Atlantic Alliance (N.A.T.O.) under the leadership of the United States, on the other Moscow and its satellites. It is true that the famous Iron Curtain speech Churchill had made at Fulton, Missouri in March, 1946 had already mentioned the division of the world into these two camps. It is also true that President Truman, as far back as March 11th, 1947 had proclaimed the so-called "Truman Doctrine", clearly defining the antagonisms existing between Soviet ambitions and United States policies, and had expressed the determination of the United States to resist aggression as far away as Greece, and to assist all free people against the imposition of totalitarian regimes. The Marshall Plan had been announced in a Harvard speech on June 5th, 1947 by General George Marshall and there had been many other statements on both sides of the Iron Curtain which had made the division actually a political truism.

Yet when Adenauer, as a German leader, touched upon the disunity amongst the Allies and established these very same premises, it generated a sense of shock. Worse was to come.

Adenauer proceeded to challenge the administration about the policy of dismantling German industry. While this policy was essentially aimed at the prevention of a German war potential, he argued, it was instead being pursued merely to impede German economic rehabilitation. In this way it was jeopardising the effectiveness of the Marshall Plan and retarding general European recovery. He cited as an example the British dismantling of the Kolibri hair comb factory, naming the British officer who had decreed it and stating that this officer was the owner of a similar and competitive hair comb business in Britain. He quoted British newspaper reports according to which British watch manufacturers had sent congratulations to the British authorities on dismantling watch manufacturing facilities in Germany, underlining the felicitous results for the British watch manufacturers who were now profiting from a rising British export market. Adenauer brought out statistics on the spread of venereal disease in connection with the armies of occupation. Economic dislocation he said was prolonging unnecessary poverty, bringing in its wake tuberculosis and other health deteriorations through malnutrition, which constituted a menace not only for Germany, but for her neighbours. Adenauer pleaded for peace, and disciplined Allied forces in Germany instead of an army of occupation, and for the establishment of domestic administration in German hands in order to cope with those problems effectively as soon as possible. He warned against the danger of internal stagnation in the political life of Germany, which might lead to extremism instead of democracy. Above all he uttered a fervent plea for the early establishment of European unification, and he caused some surprise by his conciliatory tone towards the French administration of the Saar industries, stating that even if it meant present hardship for Germany, it contained the germ of a constructive approach to a common future, along lines which would solve not only the problems of the Saar, but benefit all countries by the possible extension of joint administrations in future. It was here that he touched on possibilities later to be formulated by Robert Schuman in his plan.

Adenauer was bitterly attacked in Britain both for his accusations regarding dismantling of German industries, and for "political impertinence". Equally bitter attacks followed from the German Socialists and Nationalists for his conciliatory words on the question of the Saar. After a few days of storm at home and abroad, time for proper consideration produced the results for which Adenauer had hoped. With the problems brought into the open instead of merely being argued between himself and his colleagues on the German Parliamentary Council on the one hand, and himself and the military authorities on the other, things began to move ahead.

On April 10th, not quite a fortnight later, the military governors handed Adenauer the first definite statement of conditions considered by the three occupying powers as essential to the establishment of the so-called German Basic Law. This statement actually incorporated the decision of a foreign ministers' conference of the three allied countries, and defined the respective fields of competence as between a German Government and Parliament and the Military Allied Control Commission, which was to retain certain rights of an occupying military power. It also specified the type of parliamentary regime envisaged by the Allies for Germany. It was not all that Adenauer had hoped for, but at least it was the first concrete formulation pointing a way towards a speedy establishment of a civilian German political authority with some power of internal administration, and was a workable scheme. Evaluating time against details, Adenauer urged acceptance. But he did not know that a political surprise was in store for him.

The acceptance of the Allied proposal by his own party, the C.D.U., required some effort because of certain unsavoury aspects, but Adenauer finally obtained it. As President of the Council he also had to obtain acceptance from the other parties before the Allies would consider the scheme ratified for implementation. To everybody's surprise Kurt Schumacher, the Socialist leader, refused to make any definite decision before a meeting of his Socialist party, supposed to be held shortly at Hanover in preparation for an election, after the Basic Law had been established. When the Socialist party met, Schumacher denounced the accord as "utterly and completely unacceptable".

While Adenauer had advocated acceptance despite its insufficiencies and had argued that it was essential to hold general elections in Germany at the earliest possible date, Kurt Schumacher with studied vehemence denounced the provisions as insufficient. With a self-assurance bordering on arrogance, he accused Adenauer and his C.D.U. party of servility towards the Allies, lack of zeal in furthering German interests, and demanded certain changes. Adenauer feared interminable delays would be caused by new negotiations with the Allies, to deal with the points Schumacher had brought up. But a second surprise was in the offing.

To Adenauer's utter amazement the High Commissioners of the Allied Control Commission produced, almost immediately after Schumacher had enumerated certain demands, another document incorporating agreement with the entire list of points Schumacher had insisted upon. The Socialist press was not slow to declare this a great triumph for Schumacher. He had succeeded where Adenauer had failed. As a general election was now imminent after the Allies had accepted Schumacher's points, it put the Socialist leader in a very strong position in the eyes of the German public. Schumacher, the German champion, should become German chancellor, not, as Schumacher had formulated, "the Chancellor of the Allies", Konrad Adenauer.

There were some misgivings when it was learned that apparently the Allies had prepared a second set of proposals, should the first one prove unacceptable. It was felt by C.D.U. friends that Adenauer, as President of the Parliamentary Council, should have been treated more frankly by the Allies, at least by indicating that certain points were open for discussion.

Despite the urgings of his party followers to protest and to demand an explanation of the fact that both documents were dated April 10th, although the second document was only handed to Adenauer on April 22nd, the day after Schumacher issued his ultimatum, Adenauer remained silent, had his party ratify the second draft and then plunged into an election campaign marked by considerable anxiety in the ranks of the C.D.U., their leader apparently having been outmanoeuvred by the Socialists in such an important matter as dealing with the Allies.

Adenauer, however, seemed to have only one preoccupation, and that was to get the Basic Law ratified by the various Lands (provinces), and its second version was ratified by all the Lands, except Bavaria. This ensured the necessary two thirds majority and the new Constitution for a Federal Republic was solemnly proclaimed on May 23rd, 1949. With the work of the Parliamentary Council complete Adenauer felt free to devote his full energies to an election which was to establish the first Federal Parliament, elect the first German Government and set Germany on the arduous road to recovery.

With his political image vastly enhanced as the man who had successfully defied the Allied generals, Kurt Schumacher opened his campaign by announcing "There will be no cringing either before a French general or a Roman cardinal". This was a shot aimed directly at Konrad Adenauer's acceptance of the first proposals of the High Commissioners, and also at his well known religious affiliations; it was to be one of many such attacks. But Adenauer had only been biding his time. On July 22nd, just three weeks before polling day, Adenauer stepped onto the platform of a mass meeting held in Heidelberg. About half-way through a fairly routine electioneering appeal, he suddenly switched to the events of the previous April. This is how Weymar records the incident in Adenauer's biography:

"Calmly Adenauer told the meeting that, about a week before the Hanover (Socialist) Conference, the Executive Committee of the Social Democratic party had been confidentially informed that the Allies would not insist on their recommendations and that the Foreign Ministers Conference in Washington was prepared to meet German wishes with regard to a strengthened position of the Central Government authority in the future Federal Republic. (It will be recalled that Adenauer stood for a weakening of the central authority in favour of the provinces, while the Socialists were insisting upon a strong centralised government.)

" 'This information', Adenauer declared, raising his voice, 'was imparted to the representatives of the Social Democratic party by a high-ranking officer of the British Military Government at Headquarters in Frankfurt as early as April 14th, while I, as President of the Parliamentary Council, did not receive the news until April 20th.' Actually, a new draft was handed to Adenauer on April 22nd.

"That was a sensation indeed! It was now clear that the second letter from the three foreign ministers which General Clay had kept in his desk had been known to the Socialist party executives, at least in its essentials, before they sat down to take their 'far-reaching decisions'. Now that 'act of liberation' of the Socialists of Hanover appeared in a highly dubious light.

"The outcry of indignation which arose the very next day from the Socialist camp proved that Adenauer had hit the bull's eye. Schumacher was outraged. He called Adenauer a liar. The British authorities denied having given any prior information to the

Socialist party executive. In the face of these direct denials and accusations, Adenauer reacted by revealing his sources. The Secretary of the C.D.U. party, Herbert Blankenhorn, called a press conference. There he disclosed the fact that a British officer, indignant over the way in which members of the Labour party in England had passed the information to the German Socialists in order to give them a trump card for the coming election campaign, had fully informed Blankenhorn on what had really happened. Shortly after this disclosure the British Foreign Office took official note of the incident. Its spokesman admitted that 'on April 14th, at Frankfurt, certain indications had been given to representatives of the Social Democratic party regarding the version of the Basic Law which, in the British view, could still in an extreme case, count on an approval by the Allies'. An American newspaper wrote at the time: 'If ridicule could kill, there should now be a great many dead among the Socialist executive at Hanover' ".

It was well known that Adenauer as President of the Parliamentary Council had laboured patiently, gradually gaining one point after another in hour-long, day-long and night-long negotiations, and it was felt he had deserved better than this last minute double cross by the British Labour government and its leader Clement Attlee. Schumacher, who had been posing as a hero, was revealed as the liar he had branded Konrad Adenauer. His great defiance of the Allied Control Commission took on the appearance of a cheap electioneering trick and, above all, revealed him as the stooge of a foreign government. The subsequent newspaper headlines more than offset any favourable publicity Schumacher had received earlier. They ranged from "An impostor exposed" to "And who is the foreign stooge now?" Those who had previously urged Adenauer to protest in April realised that he had been gathering the facts before timing his reply with the master touch of a practiced politician.

Yet Adenauer's first election victory was a fairly narrow one; even with a coalition government he literally only squeezed in, particularly when it came to his own election as Chancellor, when he was elected by the new Parliament with a majority of one, doubtless his own vote. It was in the second election of 1953, that the appeal of his policies really earned him a resounding success. The C.D.U. won an absolute majority with 244 seats out of a total of 447. With his coalition partners Adenauer now controlled 307 votes. The Communists lost all their seats in the second election and disappeared from Parliament. The Socialists had only polled eight million votes against the C.D.U.'s 12.5 million, thus increasing Adenauer's lead of only eight seats in the first Parliament to ninety-four seats in the second. Adenauer was thus well placed as he entered a most crucial period of negotiations with the Allies. At that time he was seventy-eight years old.

Despite the difficulties Adenauer had had with the British military authorities while the Labour government held sway in London, the return of Churchill to power saw a considerable change; a great understanding replaced earlier friction. Adenauer visited London in 1951, and a lengthy exchange of views with Churchill and Eden at Number 10 Downing Street did much to establish common ground.

Thus we have seen that De Gasperi, Adenauer and Schuman began their domestic political tasks after World War II facing not dissimilar obstacles. None seemed to have the sympathy of the newly installed authorities in their homelands, were they foreign military government as in Italy and Germany, or military rulers as in France. Not one of the three had a political party organisation to fall back on. In each case, the party organisation of the Marxists had material and political resources of formidable potency behind them. The Communists could draw on Moscow, and the socialists, specially in Germany, received both material aid as well as political support from the occupying military in the British Zone, as well as from the British representative on the Allied Control Commission.

Only in the minds of the basically a-historic peace planners, represented by men such as Franklin Roosevelt and his associates, Harry Hopkins, Henry Morgenthau and John Winant (the latter committing suicide in a fit of despondency when he saw hopes of Soviet friendship frustrated over Berlin), could a post-war Europe be reconstituted as a kind of Rooseveltian New Deal. France, Germany and Italy each had their historic reality to contend with, a reality which was as rooted in yesterday as it was indicative of tomorrow.

Each of the key countries faced the challenge of immediate physical survival—the provision of food. But each faced also a heritage of national disgrace for political events: France's collapse and military defeat by the Germans, Italy's years under Mussolini and Germany's under Hitler. Each of these countries brought into the post-war era a record of individual heroism, as well as cruel and unjust suffering by thousands of individual citizens which long predated not only liberation, but even allied hostility to Hitler and Mussolini. The first move was naturally to reconstitute the political force in their respective countries. Once this had been achieved and they could both assume responsibility as well as justify and discharge it, the primary preoccupation was to provide the minimum of tolerable conditions in their shattered territories. Only when each assumed the position of prime minister could they hope to build beyond their homeland the Europe for which they hoped. By 1950 each had achieved that position and two of them held, or were to hold, the portfolio of Foreign Affairs. The stage was now set for their efforts towards a better international future.

CHAPTER XII

A New Europe is Born

A UNITED Europe, as envisaged by Adenauer, De Gasperi and Schuman, which would save the Free World from collapse and Communist domination, encompassed three points. Integration into a federated system, along political, economic and military lines, involving the sacrifice of absolute national sovereignty, was their objective.

First, the political line was attempted and although this proved almost to be putting the cart before the horse, it had considerable merit for the future. It created the Council of Europe and the European Parliament, later to meet at Strasbourg. If its deliberations did not seem to show tangible results, it offered a platform for the meeting of nations no longer divided into vanquished and victors, and their very discussions revealed difficulties and possibilities which, when properly studied, could be overcome and further exploited.

When the political approach revealed the insurmountable difficulties of getting down to practical working measures, Robert Schuman came up with the second possibility, economic integration; a merging of interlocking interests, the abolition of trade barriers eliminating economic competition between rival countries which in the past had led to fatal political conflicts. The working-out of common policies for use of the labour market by interchangeable equalised social benefits between countries, freedom of movement for workers to seek employment and a gradual strengthening of joint economic policies, could never be implemented without political integration as an inevitable corollary in the long run.

The third step was in the European Defence Community, the E.D.C., the establishment of a joint defence force, a plan launched by René Pleven when he was Prime Minister and Robert Schuman, Foreign Minister of France.

Both economic and military plans were launched by France, and although she herself finally rejected the defence proposals accepted by everyone else involved, the economic plan has survived the dangerous strain imposed by the policies of General de Gaulle, and there is room for hope that it has retained enough vitality to develop, expand and eventually lead to the political and military integration which seems inevitable as an alternative to disaster.

Obviously, like all historical events, these three plans long pre-dated in their general concept their actual formulations, for there were many who strove patiently towards those ends over many years. We have seen how Robert Schuman welcomed diplomatic moves for a European, and particularly for a Franco-German understanding under Aristide Briand in the early 1930's. The work done by Count Coudenhove-Kallergi, son of an Austrian diplomat and a Japanese mother, for a united Europe had enthusiastic supporters in many European countries before World War I, particularly among statesmen.

On May 5th, 1949, when De Gasperi addressed the first European Parliament in the Palace of Europe in Strasbourg, it was generally acclaimed that he had provided the basic idea on which post-war peace could be built. Above all he underlined the absolute necessity of a joint ideal of unity, and a substitute for the dangerous spirit of nationalism, the cause of so much evil. He pointed out that Italy was one of the nations which had lost the war, and with it many of her illusions. He developed his idea further when he spoke to the same assembly on December 10th, 1951 and said: "The condition essential for a resistance of Europe against outside enemies is a defence against the ominous inheritance of civil war. That is what we must consider a European war to be from the point of view of universal history: this alternating of aggressions and re-vindications, the spirit of hegemony, avidity for riches and for space, the anarchy and tyranny which our history has recorded together with its glorious past". It was against "germs of disintegration and decline, reciprocal distrust and moral disintegration" that Europeans had to struggle.

"What is the alternative which presents itself to us in this post-war period?", De Gasperi asked the Assembly. "We are all agreed that we must defend our homesteads, our institutions, our civilisation, which are in such peril at the moment. But the new generations, which seek an integrated concept and dynamism of life, hesitate before the choice which might decide their destiny. Are they to take that road which has already been strewn with revindications and with conflicts inspired by a concept of absolute nationality, or are they to go along the road of coordinated forces? Is one to follow ideals rationally or follow the other road of the instinctive and the irrational? Is one to seek greater expansion or a wider fraternity and solidarity?"

The building of national understanding was not easy, but De Gasperi's preparation was a great asset. Well versed in history, he also had the experience of years of statesmanship when he had been defending the rights of nationality without having been a nationalist. This was underlined in 1952 when he was the recipient of the Charles the Great Prize conferred on "the most eminent European" at Aachen. He was active in mediating between Schuman and Adenauer on the thorny question of the Saar, because he believed in the absolute necessity of co-operation between Germany and France, and he was combating the efforts of Moscow to divide Europeans from the store of his own experience. In 1952 Pietro Nenni, the then pro-Communist leader of the Italian Socialist party, who in 1969 broke with some of his own Socialists because they wanted to follow the Moscow line, came back from Moscow with Stalin's suggestion of a non-aggression pact with Italy, rather than have Italy tie herself to N.A.T.O. in close co-operation with her Western neighbours and friends. In a biting reply to the lure of neutrality which Nenni was expounding in the Italian parliament, De Gasperi warned against the efforts of Moscow to wean Italy from the European Pact. He bade Nenni remember that Moscow had a long record of non-aggression pacts, always preliminaries to Moscow aggression. He reminded the Italian parliament of the non-aggression pact with Finland in 1932, preparatory to the Red Army's attack on that country; the non-agression pact signed with Poland which was then partitioned by Soviet Russia, with the help of Hitler, seven years later. There was a non-agression pact, De Gasperi recalled, with Rumania in 1933 and an occupation of Rumania's province of Bessarabia a few years later. Lithuania, Estonia and Latvia were given non-aggression pacts by Moscow in 1939 and only a few months later they were occupied by Soviet troops and were incorporated into the Soviet Union.

When Nenni replied that he saw no difference in fact between a non-aggression pact with Moscow and the Atlantic Pact and N.A.T.O., De Gasperi shot back that Palmiro Togliatti, the Communist leader in parliament, was at least more sincere. He had earlier propounded to the Italian Parliament exactly the same proposal, obviously from Stalin, but had called it an "alternative" policy for Italy, because he, Togliatti, definitely saw the difference.

As De Gasperi was championing the cause of international understanding, Dean Acheson urged him to press forward for Europe, assuring him that "France, Germany and Anglo-Americans will follow you". Being a realist, however, De Gasperi never lost himself in "global dreams" of world government, or in illusions of building international world superstructures without consolidating regional bases of understanding, to give them sound foundations. That is why Europe and such structures as the European Common Market became his most direct preoccupation.

But De Gasperi was building to assure peace for Europe, not aggression against the East, and he strove through his embassies and his speeches to keep the door open to understanding with Eastern neighbours; he was providing the door, and good locks for it, as security against their aggression.

European integration and an eventual understanding with the East, were also the dominant aims of Konrad Adenauer. The first was referred to in his memoirs when he said: "I am a German, but I am and I have always felt myself to be a European. That is why I have from the very start devoted myself to an understanding with France, without which Europe is simply not possible. I have stood for that during twenty years of political crises (of the former Reich government). . . . Already after the First World War I advocated an organic intertwining of French, Belgian and German industry in order to assure a lasting peace. I did this because, according to my conviction, a parallel developed and coordinated industrial interest is the surest and most lasting foundation for political relations between people and will always continue to be so." This idea was originated in 1922 and it eventually was to find expression in the Schuman Plan and the European Common Market. In the Stresemann papers referred to by Fritz Stern in his article in the *Political Science Quarterly* of March, 1958, Konrad Adenauer, then Lord Mayor of Cologne, is quoted as saying to the Chairman of the Allied Rhineland Commission, at the very height of the Ruhr crisis, "A lasting peace between France and Germany can only be attained through the establishment of a community of economic interest between the two countries".

Adenauer was preoccupied with something he believed to be rooted in the character, history and geography of the many branches of the German people. Their location in the heart of Europe made it inevitable, he seemed to think, that throughout the centuries there was no possible development on the Continent without involvement of the Germanic tribes, be they Franks or Swabians, Saxons or Allemanns or, for that matter, Lombards, Goths or Vandals. Their tribalism left them divided into innumerable earldoms, dukedoms and even kingdoms, ready to join with powerful neighbours, Huns, Byzantines or Romans, even against each other if circumstances seemed to warrant it, or else to coalesce against a third party. All such inter-German alliances were temporary with frequently changing partners. Only in modern times, with the emergence of Prussia as a subsidised anti-Austrian satellite of

France in the eighteenth century, did the first stronger Germanic political structure emerge. Austria, despite its German Habsburg rulers, never pretended to be a German state, but rather a heterogeneous empire, centrally directed, with an Austro-German minority, powerful around the throne, but part of a majority of Bohemians, Hungarians, Slavs, Mohammedans, Bulgarians, Swiss and Italian people, all part of a Habsburg realm. An emerging German political state-consciousness in Europe became apparent well after more clearly structured English, French, Spanish and Portuguese political empires had emerged under ruling dynasties.

The Germans were in a way the Johnnies-come-lately. Whether they looked to the West, the North-West, across the English channel or South at Austria, they saw maturer state-structures. But looking eastward, the Germans found that their somewhat retarded political adolescence was comparatively mature as against the disjointed dynastic and political progress of Poland, Russia and her borderlands, and of the crumbling Turkish empire.

Twelve centuries of emigration by German people into those Eastern areas had left their mark; the establishment in the thirteenth century of the Brethren of the Sword in the Baltics, or earlier German merchants settling in Novgorod and Moscow; later migrations of German peasants settling on the Volga or in the Ukraine, were all at the request of and encouraged by Russian rulers, who wanted capable agriculturists, artisans and, later on, industrialists. To many Germans the East had the fascination of adventure, fortune and future. First traced in the eighteenth century and promoted with skill and success by Bismarck in the nineteenth century was a foreign policy trend of a nascent German state seeking political alignments eastward.

This was what Adenauer knew only too well. He remembered the Treaty of Rapallo in 1922, when a defeated Germany joined forces with Bolshevik-ruled Russia to vitiate the Versailles Treaty. He remembered how General von Seekt clandestinely rebuilt a German army on Russian soil with weapons which had been prohibited by the Western Allies under the terms of the Versailles Treaty. It was the old attraction of the East for Germans, an attraction to join if not to conquer, which he realised to be a potent factor and effective propaganda weapon in Moscow's hands. If the West proved too intransigent and too harsh in its treatment of a conquered Germany, there was always the East as an alternative. As Adenauer once implied in a conversation with me, if he could not achieve a union between France and Germany to safeguard a united Europe—to which Russia and other countries of Eastern Europe could eventually adhere—then a frustrated Germany under a different government than his own might join Russia and help to destroy what the Western world had acquired in freedom, human dignity and spiritual heritage through the centuries.

Thus Adenauer's motives for a Franco-German understanding, and his fear of a German drift into the Eastern orbit, were in a way serving the same purpose, to implement his great vision of a European federation, which could only be made to work when Germany and France were reconciled.

All federations obviously imply a renunciation of sovereign rights. It was on August 13th, 1950 that Robert Schuman, defending his plan before the assembly at Strasbourg, said: "I accept the principle of a renunciation of sovereign rights, not by themselves, not as an end in itself, but as a necessity, as the only means of overcoming national egotism, the antagonisms and narrowness of mind which destroyed us".

"We do not intend to be presumptuous when we say that the proposals which have been made and have been accepted, once they are realised the way they have been accepted, imply eventualities we cannot yet gauge, but which will rapidly develop in the sense of a complete unification of Europe, economically and politically".

History makes it practically impossible to fix exact dates marking the beginning of an era or even of an event. All historical happenings are happenings to humans, caused by human actions, influenced or even shaped by earlier causes. Ignorance of sequences still does not validate a childhood proposition, favoured to-day by so-called calendar people, those who remain immature despite their calendar age, which classifies them as adults. To these people of adult age, but immature mind, it is not sequences of history but merely the rather childish assertion, "This is so because it is so" that matters.

Hence arbitrary dates are fixed as a mere convenience for the beginning or end of an era or a political system. The rise and fall of the Roman empire, the beginning of feudalism, the birth of democracy, a post-war or a pre-war era, depend on the historian rather than on exact chronology. History, like a stream, flows from and winds on far beyond the horizon of an individual who himself remains limited in time and space at a fixed point somewhere along the changing vistas. A specific occurrence, like a battle, a birth or death of a ruler, the outbreak of a revolution, is merely a date in history which can never be evaluated out of a wider context.

Perhaps the date of the first European Parliament on May 5th, 1949 in the Palace of Europe in Strasbourg can conveniently be taken to mark the turning point in the immediate post-war struggle for survival of the Free World. The danger of a third world war to destroy the victorious Red Army, which was ready to feed the puppet Communist parties in the heart of Europe, began to wane earlier with the establishment of strong, popular regimes led by the three men who had most clearly foreseen and prepared to meet the challenge.

Obviously Adenauer oversimplified, as was his wont, and his special gift on the political hustings, when I once asked him for a quick definition of his basic policies. "Do you know the Junior Catechism (Kleiner Katechismus)?" he asked. "It contains what I believe and hence all my political objectives can be found there". As to his methods, he added that improvisation was always necessary in politics. In a way he was echoing what, maybe in different words, Schuman and Adenauer would also have replied.

It is not surprising, therefore, that the quest for a supra-national structure which would curtail the sovereignty of their individual nations by merging into a federated Europe, the establishment of a common market and a joint defence force attracted and animated these three men. By their very beliefs they were opposed, and diametrically opposed, to nineteenth century concepts of absolute sovereignty.

They also knew that just as the amputation of a fox-terrier's tail cannot make short tails hereditary for the breed, no act of politics, be it ever so guilty, can carry the guilt concept across generations. The notion of "national guilt" is basically a figment of political imagination or mendacious demagogy which appeals to man's meaner instinct of anger and revenge. While it is true that the sins of the father shall be visited upon his children, it is equally true that each child will accept such visitation as nothing more than a personal misfortune, not as something to be dutifully expiated, but rather resentfully suffered and rapidly replaced by efforts to mend his lot.

Hence each of the three men, as soon as his own political position permitted, was determined to safeguard his people's future by eliminating those factors which had been the cause of succeeding national disasters. It was obvious that the principal cause could be found in applying a byzantine concept of absolute sovereignty to a modern political and often accidental collective called a "state". A state might at best enjoy certain sovereign privileges, but never absolute rights. As Innocent III in the thirteenth century had challenged the absolute right of a monarch, claiming that the Emperor could only exercise certain privileges bestowed by the only absolute authority—God, so Catholic teaching throughout the centuries maintained, as Thomas More had maintained even unto death, that he was the King's good servant but God's first.

Henry VIII had to decapitate Sir Thomas, because he was convinced that the Tudor lineage gave him as King the absolute right, a right not merely based on might, but on justice, for he gave Thomas More a trial. There the principle was established that for a subject to challenge the absolute right of the King by the claim that the King was in fact challenging the laws of God, was a breach of that loyalty to the King which could be demanded of a subject. Because of his religious convictions, Sir Thomas had inevitably to challenge such a claim, which ran counter to the teachings of the Church in all ages.

It was therefore no accident that throughout history the claims of Caesar, whether his name was Constantine or Theodoric, Attila or Lenin, Napoleon I or Hitler, Peter the Great or the modern technocrat, were always being challenged by Catholic teaching which in turn claimed the Law of God as the only supreme source of all law. By the same token it was only logical that all absolute political rulers, be they individual dictators imposing their will on the citizens under totalitarian regimes, or champions of absolute sovereignty in the dealings of one state with the other, had to single out the Church as their most obvious enemy. This was as true and as imperative for a Communist power in the Kremlin as it was for Bismarck's ambitions in a *Kulturkampf* or for the modern state's impatience with religion in schools, lest it lead to the questioning of the rectitude of some, even democratic, legislation.

Thus when the first European meeting took place in the spring of 1949, one could consider it as a turning point in the immediate post-war struggle, because the survival of the beliefs of De Gasperi, Schuman and Adenauer seemed more certain.

De Gasperi was in solid political control in Italy, the Peace Treaty having been signed on February 10th, 1948; the occupation of Trieste was ended on March 20th, 1949 and the elections of April 18th, 1948 had given his Christian Democratic Party 300 seats and his government a comfortable majority in a free parliament.

In France, Robert Schuman had firmly established his position, having been named Prime Minister in November, 1947 and he exerted considerable influence also in the subsequent years as Foreign Minister.

Konrad Adenauer had completed the organisation of his party of Christian Democrat and Social Union, and on April 22nd, 1949 the formal draft of the Basic Law, providing for free elections and the establishment of a German government named by parliament, had been hammered out for ratification.

Thus when the European Parliament met, all three statesmen could join in the first deliberations as men seeking common ground for a common future in freedom and hope for peace. That it was these three men who played a very particular role, was confirmed by no less a person than Paul Henri Spaak who was the leader, as Foreign Minister and later as Prime Minister of Belgium, of his people both in exile and in his re-established country after Nazi liberation. When the first Council of Europe met on August 10th, 1949 in Strasbourg and elected Spaak as its first President, he recalls in his memoirs *Combats Inachevés*[1] that it was a period of great enthusiasm and adds: "Adenauer, Schuman, De Gasperi and Jean Monet were our *chefs de file*. At one time following their lead, at another urging them on, we made progress towards that Europe of which we were all dreaming. It was exhilarating".

It soon proved that the "all" to which Spaak referred did not include too many. Already the next year, during the second session, Spaak recalls, Harold Macmillan for Britain, supported by the Scandinavian Countries, made it clear that they were not sharing the same enthusiasm. They were not interested in a federated Europe which could include them. Macmillan gave a speech in which he differentiated between the pragmatic approach of the English who would like to build from experience towards a principle, "the method of Bacon and Newton", as he called it, which was opposed, he said, "to the Continental tradition which likes to reason *a priori* and descend from the summit towards the plain, starting from a general principle in order to arrive at its political application. That is the tradition of Thomas Acquinas, the scholastics and the great Continental thinkers". Macmillan continued his argument by pointing out that:

"Our people will not cede to a supra-national authority to close our mines or our steel mills. Our people will not permit a supranational authority to reduce to unemployment a large portion of our fellow citizens of Durham, the Midlands or South Wales or Scotland. These fears might be illusory but their existence, is in fact, a fact that no British government can ignore".

This was echoed in Europe by General de Gaulle, who broke the silence from his retirement at Colombey-les-deux-Eglises, by addressing the mayors of Robert Schuman's constituency of the Moselle. In characteristic, somewhat bombastic rhetoric he said:

"When Schuman says, 'It is necessary to construct a new economy', the proposal is put forth for a hodge-podge of coal and steel, invoking a union of some sort, without knowing where one is going."

Paul Henri Spaak, who was a great enthusiast, not only because he was President, but also as a great proponent of European

[1] *Combats Inachevés*, Henri Spaak, (Fayard, Paris).

understanding, recalls a speech by Michel Debré (later to become one of de Gaulle's most trusted ministers under the Fifth Republic in which he held the Prime Ministership for many years), in which he was in "complete isolation" within the French Delegation in opposing the plan. "At the time that was but the expression of a French minority opinion which gathered together the Communists and the extreme right", Spaak comments. That he, the Socialist, did not quite accurately gauge the opposition can be seen from the fact that his own fellow Socialists in Germany were bitterly attacking Adenauer and his pro-European efforts.

When on May 9th, 1950 Robert Schuman, in the course of a press conference in the Salle d'Horloge at the Quay d'Orsay, made the dramatic announcement proposing the merger of the coal and steel industries of France, Germany, Luxembourg, Holland, Belgium and Italy under the jurisdiction of a high authority, although he risked his own political future, he exhibited a political dexterity few people had suspected this taciturn and somewhat retiring politician of possessing.

There was no doubt that the Council of Europe, and in particular the European Parliament, was unable at that point to be much more than a political platform or sounding board. But the longer it resounded with speeches made by political leaders not speaking to each other but to their home constituencies, the more that early enthusiasm of which Paul Henri Spaak had spoken was eroded.

They wanted to impress with their erudition as well as with their orthodoxy and with well-tried but outworn political banalities. They were all for peace and understanding in principle, but for no possible action which would permit their people to participate in concrete measures limiting their countries' sovereignty in favour of a supra-national authority. They were all afraid of accusations of disloyalty, especially in France where de Gaulle's displeasure was a factor to be reckoned with.

Men of goodwill, committed to a better future, grew desperate, seeing a once recovering Europe now rapidly slithering back into old political patterns for which the entire world had paid with untold suffering in two murderous conflicts within the last few decades.

Adenauer and De Gasperi consulted and tried to press for concrete action, but they also realised that as representatives of countries officially among the vanquished, they could not be decisive in initiating a new policy, only supporting it. The United States was pressing for concrete action, because it saw the great economic benefit of recovery initiated by the Marshall Plan in jeopardy unless the next step toward greater European cooperation could be taken. But the United States could not take an initiative for

European nations. She was an outsider incapable, for domestic reasons, of joining in a common market of political unification. Congress would never accept any limitations on its rights of decision. Great Britain approved of a European economic consolidation in a rather abstract form, provided she could stay out, and also provided no move conjured up the spectre of a dreaded "continental block" too potent for Britain's still cherished policy of retaining the balance of power, able to balance the scales between continental coalitions.

Thus the only country that could move with any hope of achievement was France, and Schuman fully realised it.

It was a difficult moment for France. The war in Indo-China was threatening the stability of the economy as well as the political equilibrium by its drain both on men and resources, coupled with serious military reverses.

In efforts to revive the German economy and rehabilitation, the United States was pressing France to abandon a purely negative attitude since stagnation in Germany, it was now apparent, inhibited European recovery. The United States and Britain considerably relaxed occupation measures in Germany, and France was facing the danger of being isolated by her allies who were in fact assisting German recovery, a fact Frenchmen dreaded but could not hinder.

Thus Schuman, as a Frenchman, was deeply aware that his country's interests made it imperative to extricate France from that sterile policy, so dramatically associated with de Gaulle and summed up in his favourite political expression, "Non". And Schuman, the world statesman and fervent European, was equally convinced that unless Germany and France could find a new approach to peaceful co-existence, all the talk at Strasbourg and elsewhere of the peaceful building of a viable future would remain just talk.

So there was Schuman, the man from Lorraine and a specialist in economic policies: he knew that there was a complementary situation between Germany's Ruhr and Saar coal and the Minette iron-ore deposits of his native Lorraine. Steelmills in Lorraine and in the Ruhr and the Saar, were operating with German coal and French Minette iron-ore, after the English process (the Gilchrist-Thomas smelting techniques) had made Minette ore a potential for a grade of steel comparable to the Swedish and other ores. Belgian and Luxembourg mines, together with the mines of north-eastern France and north-western Germany, constituted the famous "Triangle" of heavy industry, which was in fact the industrial heart of Europe. It was for that reason the centre of the German (Krupp, etc.) and French (Schneider-Creuzot) armament industries, supplying each country with its sinews of war—to be used against each other. That was one of the reasons why in 1870 Germany had annexed Schuman's native Lorraine and why France in 1918 and again in 1945 tried to possess or at least control Germany's Saar and Ruhr areas. Here was something that nature and geography had joined together which man at his peril had tried to tear asunder for years, and if that complex could ever be put under joint and common control, to be developed for the benefit of all concerned, one of the long standing causes of war would be eliminated. Schuman, the Lorrainer, and Adenauer, the Rhinelander, had lived with the knowledge of that problem and realised that only its solution could lead to a real and durable understanding in other fields. Already in 1926, an international cartel of the steel producers and hence coal-users of France, Germany, Belgium and Luxembourg had been formed. Gustav Stresemann welcomed it as a forerunner of greater international cooperation, but it broke down under national rivalries, with governments helping rather than moderating the competitive ambitions of their national industries, Germans out-producing French in a scramble for the world market.

There were two schools of thought amongst the many favouring a merger of the coal and steel industries of France and Germany and the so-called Be-Ne-Lux countries, Belgium, Netherlands and Luxembourg. One supported the expropriation of existing owners and the creation of a giant trust. Here one finds such economists as Barbara Ward, who referred to a "public steel corporation", in her book *The West at Bay*,[1] the French Socialist André Philippe who advocated collective ownership, the German Socialists advocating nationalisation, and a Heidelberg Action Group around Alfred Weber also advocating nationalisation, but always with each nation retaining control over its unit. There were many more who all recognised the common purpose which should be pursued, but all missed a cardinal point which emerged clearly from the policy being pursued by Schuman and Adenauer, and also De Gasperi who now played a great role in smoothing out French-German differences.

The other school led by these three contended that all national cartels, despite socialisation of the industries in these countries, were still individual national measures. It was not domestic industries which had to be regulated, but national policies in regard to the industries which had to be curbed. In fact, the real "hot potato", which had been avoided till then, was how to create, not

[1] *The West at Bay*, Barbara Ward (Allen & Unwin, London).

merely an industrial complex jointly managed, but a supra-national body which would be strong enough to control and direct national policy in respect of industry in the various countries. It was a question of voluntarily relinquishing certain sovereign rights to a supra-national body. Harold Macmillan saw clearly that what was really involved was, as he said, ceding to a supra-national authority the right to close "our mines and our steel mills". Hence Britain at that time had refused to accept any vital limitations. Yet precisely this right was more important than the formal ownership of any national industry.

Thus the problem was not merely an economic arrangement to bring the economic advantages inherent in economic cooperation: it involved an immense and unique break-through in political unification by removing from purely national control a vital national economic factor which too frequently strengthened, and even encouraged, national intransigence. Instead of heavy industry serving its own narrow national interests, and often subsidising political nationalism to the point of aggressive expansionism, a supra-national authority was to be endowed with an economic complex which could exert continued influence towards a wider economic and political union, a common market, the disappearance of passports and residential restrictions, establishment of currency parity etc., etc., all tending inevitably towards political union.

In a study in economic cooperation *The Schuman Plan*[1]—William J. Diebold Jr. writes:

"This was a drastic change in the direction of French policies. It caught foreigners and Frenchmen by surprise. Such speed, in contrast to the long and slow exchanges of views, mulling, and cautious drafting that normally precede major shifts in policy, inevitably raised questions about motive, sincerity and feasibility. No one could say how far the Assembly and the French people would back the foreign minister, even if foreign governments—for whom the implications were also drastic—proved responsive. Yet there was a clear, basic logic. France could not prevent the growth of German strength; to try to delay that growth would weaken France's position; the possibility that remained was to find a new framework within which German development could proceed along channels that were not only less worrying for France, but that promised positive benefits to both countries; to serve mutual interests, France would have to make concessions and treat Germany as an equal".

There are some interesting details regarding the preparatory work in Robert Rochefort's biography of Schuman. Apparently, after

[1] *The Schuman Plan*, William J. Diebold Jr. (Frederick Praeger, New York).

several discussions, Jean Monet worked out a draft which Schuman read during the night of April 28th; he told Bernard Clappier, Chief of his Cabinet, that he was satisfied with the political aspect of the draft, but wanted to be reassured that the risks involved for the French steel industry were "not too terrible". Clappier replied that he and Monet had carefully examined that aspect, but felt the French steel industry was strong enough to face such risks.

"Think about that, it is most important", Schuman is reported as saying, "and when I return (from Metz), I shall question you further about that".

On Monday, May 1st, Clappier, burning with impatience, met Schuman at the Gare de l'Est. Schuman had spent the weekend at his country home Scy Chaselles, studying the draft. A meeting of foreign ministers in London was only a few days away. France could not arrive there without some constructive suggestion after having tried the patience of her allies by a series of sterile refusals to accept any plan for a German rehabilitation, something all were agreed on as essential for European recovery.

Schuman greeted his Chief of Cabinet and insisted, during the drive to the Quay d'Orsay, on talking only of the weather. Finally Clappier could contain himself no longer. "Monsieur le Président, the paper I gave you last Saturday, have you had time to think about it? What do you think about it?"

"Well, my answer is yes."

A few minutes later they were closeted with Monet and worked again on details of the procedure to get quick action.

At a Cabinet meeting on May 3rd, Schuman gave only a very general outline of the plan and kept rather to vague details. He emphasised the need for secrecy, so as to avoid stirring up premature opposition. Later he had to defend himself before the Legislature against attacks on precisely that point of secrecy. Schuman made a very spirited and strong defence. Citing a predecessor at the Foreign Office, Aristide Briand, who had always justified a certain initial secrecy when going into negotiations, Schuman argued that while he absolutely agreed to submit to the ultimate decision of the Legislature, he also had to assert the right of the Executive not to go into negotiations with its hands tied by previous legislative directives. "You may be sure that I always fully respect the constitutional and moral right of Parliament. But still I cannot accept that negotiations should be carried on by an assembly".

Robert Schuman informed Dean Acheson, U.S. Secretary of State, of the plan as he passed through Paris on his way to the London conference. The meeting was attended by only one other person, the United States Ambassador David Bruce, who acted as interpreter, and the talks were kept very private. Acheson, recalling the meeting on the project, later to be called the Schuman Plan, considered it was "a step towards unification of Western Europe which takes one's breath away".

On the evening of May 8th, Schuman sent an envoy to Bonn to bring the text of the plan to Konrad Adenauer. It was May 9th, in the forenoon, that the French Cabinet met, but it was only towards the end, shortly after noon, that Robert Schuman outlined the full plan. Schuman later said he had waited till then because he wanted to have Adenauer's reaction before venturing into the final battle for the plan. Only when he had received Adenauer's consent, which arrived about noon on the 9th, did he feel the struggle could commence. Since Germany was primarily involved, Schuman felt the entire proposal depended on Adenauer's support.

Apparently Bideault, then Prime Minister, who had been handed the draft of the text by Jean Monet when he worked it out with Schuman and gave Schuman a copy, had actually never read it, despite statements Bideault subsequently made to the contrary.

Jean Monet recounts that on his return from London, whither he had accompanied Schuman, Bideault called him by telephone.

"Monsieur Monet", said Bideault, "Monsieur Schuman read a text at the Cabinet meeting of a declaration. Is it not true that you had drafted it?"

Monet: "That is right".

Bideault: "I thought that text had been assigned for action to the Prime Minister's office."

Monet: "But you did not reply."

When Monet went to see Bideault after the telephone call and saw him open a drawer, "there he found the paper which he had not read".

René Mayer, at that time Privy Seal, recounts that he sat next to Bideault at the Cabinet meeting at which Schuman presented the plan, and could, therefore, closely watch Bideault's reactions.

"After the reading of a remarkable exposé by Robert Schuman, which was convincing because Schuman appeared so convinced, there was some hesitation . . . Bideault was evidently furious because he had not been appraised and was fit to explode. But maybe he remembered that at the end of a dinner at the Matignon (Palace) we, Schuman, Pleven and I, had vainly tried to have him stay a bit longer so we could talk to him about it".

Mayer then claims that he saved the day for Schuman by strongly supporting him and that Vincent Auriol, the President of the Republic, commented that he "spoke like a torrent", and that "Bideault was against the plan but then rallied to agree".

Rochefort quotes Professor Daniel Villey as saying that Bideault actually thought about resigning over the Schuman Plan. The point at issue, of course, was that the Schuman Plan was the first international agreement allowing Germany to be treated as a full-fledged and equal partner, a cardinal point towards European union, but a point on which Bideault reacted emotionally and which he rejected.

"This overwhelming and courageous initiative of Robert Schuman", Adenauer was to write later, "was a political act of extraordinary significance, assuring him a place in history among great Frenchmen and great Europeans". At the press conference on May 9th, Schuman was asked whether his concept of Europe was limited to Western Europe, "or whether Soviet Russia was also in Europe". He answered that she was. This point was again underlined by him in a debate on December 6th, 1951 before the French Assembly, when he reiterated "We must not construct a Europe sadly mutilated. We must not construct Europe only in the interests of people who are free, but must also be able to welcome the people of the East, who once freed from subjugation of which they have been the victims, will ask to join us". This, incidentally, was also a point De Gasperi and Adenauer constantly underlined. They both looked forward to the time when Eastern Europe would be able to live in freedom and peace within a united Europe.

"What we seek to achieve by a fusion of interests, by indissoluble economic ties, is the impossibility of war between the enemies of yesterday, to establish a habit of working together", Schuman told the Assembly. "That is why we remain profoundly convinced that the surest and most rapid means to achieve this is cooperation between France and Germany within a multilateral framework, where it will be possible for particularism to be mitigated by many contacts with a whole group of associates", he explained. The attacks against him were as violent from the extreme right as from the extreme left. In response to a question as to who was the ultimate winner of the battle, Schuman replied by plagiarising from a famous phrase coined by Field Marshal Joffre, when the latter was asked, "Who has actually won the battle of the Marne?" "I do not know who has won it, but I do know very well who could have lost it".

In Germany, Adenauer's opposition in Parliament when he pressed for the ratification of the Schuman Plan came primarily from the Socialists who accused him in terms familiar to the most extreme nationalists of jeopardising Germany's national independence.

Chapter XIII

The Great Bequest

World events took a drastic turn shortly after the Schuman Plan was launched, and was due to be negotiated and drafted. The outbreak of the Korean War not only shifted the United States' interests from Europe, but made war efforts more of a reality for Washington than peace endeavours. This had an immediate reaction on United States and British attitudes regarding European continental defence, a burden they both felt should be more extensively assumed by continentals themselves. This, translated into practical terms, meant a growing need for German participation in defence.

While the next French initiative, the European Defence Community (E.D.C.) was in no structural way related to the Schuman Plan there was one similarity. René Pleven, as Premier of France, and Robert Schuman, as Foreign Minister, were under increasing Allied pressure to utilise German defence resources as the Communist danger, already expressing itself in the war in Korea and also present with the Red Army at the Elbe River, was no longer a political abstraction.

Facing the inevitable changes which had to come in the defence provisions for Europe, the French borrowed the Schuman Plan formula of permitting German association, but within the wider framework of an international structure. Germany should make a contribution, not with a German army, but by furnishing men within a European army establishment.

In New York on September 12th, 1950 Dean Acheson informed a meeting of foreign ministers of United States, Great Britain and France, that the United States expected Germany to furnish twelve divisions for European defence. Schuman immediately saw the dilemma he faced: either German rearmament or the United States would pull out of Europe. He was as opposed to a German army as Adenauer himself. He suggested, in order to gain time, a consultation between the defence ministers of the three Great Powers, General Marshall, Jules Moch for France and Emmanuel

Shinwell for Britain. Count Jacques de Bourbon-Bousset, then Director of Robert Schuman's Cabinet, described this meeting of Defence Ministers to Georgette Elgey.[1] "It was a rather comic quarrel among the Socialists when Emanuel Shinwell shouted at his fellow Socialist, Jules Moch, that one had had about enough of the French putting spokes in the wheels. 'One can jolly well do without you', Shinwell exclaimed. Thereupon Jules Moch shrieked back at his British Socialist confrère: 'It is not with your divisions in Europe that you will greatly help us. One has no need of you!' Moch categorically rejected Dean Acheson's proposition and suggested instead a dialogue with Soviet Russia, which greatly annoyed Acheson."

Moch then threatened to let the Russians into Indochina. The Americans sat silent and angered. The French attitude at the meeting is credited to the British having overcome their reticence about German rearmament and siding unequivocally with the Americans. France was isolated anew. It seems Jean Monet was again the one who suggested to René Pleven the use of the Schuman Plan idea of a multilateral framework. On October 24th, 1950 Pleven proposed to the French National Assembly his plan as a way out for France. This plan called for a European army incorporating German divisions but under European command. No German army was to be established. On October 26th the debate was over, and the French National Assembly, without marked enthusiasm, accepted the Pleven proposal by 343 votes against the 255 votes of a combined Gaullist and Communist opposition.

The weakest point of the Pleven plan was the lack of enthusiasm not only of the Assembly, but also of its author, just as the political strength of the Schuman Plan was the whole hearted personal enthusiasm and total engagement of Robert Schuman in fighting for what he totally believed to be necessary. According to Adenauer's memoirs, Winston Churchill told him during his London visit, when the two discussed the E.D.C.: "What causes me concern is the lack of enthusiasm of the French. Their project is too much merely an insurance against a risk. One can never achieve anything big when one is guided by fear".

After long negotiations the E.D.C. plan was perfected into a European Defence Community. At a solemn ceremony on May 27th, 1952 the E.D.C. Treaty had been signed at the Quay d'Orsay in the Salle d'Horloge. Apart from the foreign ministers of Belgium, France, Germany, Holland, Luxembourg and Italy, Anthony

[1] Ibid.,

Eden for Great Britain signed a guarantee agreement with the six signatories, by which Britain undertook, for the duration of its membership in NATO, to come to the aid of the E.D.C. in Europe. This was followed by Dean Acheson, who did the same for the United States, and then Robert Schuman signed again for France, this time as a guarantor of the treaty and as a NATO member, the same as Great Britain and the United States. Thus France actually signed two agreements, both as a member of the E.D.C. as well as its guarantor. It was estimated that no less than 400 signatures had been affixed to the Treaty, the Treaty of Guarantee and the numerous protocols and memoranda which belonged to the entire complex.

On January 11th, 1952 Germany had ratified the Schuman Plan, and now was to proceed with the ratification of the E.D.C. and thereby be integrated into the European framework when all others had also signed. Each of these treaties and accords had caused Adenauer bitter debates and ever fiercer opposition from the Socialist and Nationalists voting together against the accords. But by August 1953 Europe had only been constructed in draft form. Europe had not yet really been unified. French cabinets changed frequently and each hesitated to ask for the ratification of the key treaty, the E.D.C. Adenauer was growing ever more anxious, fearing that German impatience with French delays would lead to the revival of a nationalist sentiment, should the ideals of a united Europe fail.

The Pleven government of 1951, the author of the E.D.C., had been defeated and was succeeded by the Pinay government in 1952. On the fall of that government, René Mayer succeeded with a coalition government into which he took the Gaullists. Before the Gaullists would join, he had to pledge re-negotiation of certain aspects of the E.D.C., particularly providing for the maintenance of the integrity of French defence with a national army. The Gaullists also insisted that the Saar future, not yet determined, was to be clarified, obviously in France's favour, before ratification of the E.D.C. would be asked for in the French National Assembly. The government of René Mayer fell with the E.D.C. still not introduced for ratification, and Laniel headed a new coalition. In order to clarify the situation for Mendès-France, who then succeeded Laniel, and at the same time to allay French fears, Adenauer gave a radio interview on July 1st, 1954 to the German journalist Ernst Friedlander, in which he repeated his beliefs that the European Defence Community would be the only practical solution.

"Of course it was possible to visualise various alternatives", Adenauer said, "but none of them appeared nearly as good".

And then he made the most pointed remark towards the French by saying, "No alternative to the E.D.C. is possible or feasible without the creation of a German national army. The German people, however, do not want a national army. We realise quite clearly that such a national army would inevitably awaken new fears and new suspicions in France. It would indeed be a political paradox if France, of all nations, were to compel us through her procrastination to create a German national army which she herself fears more than anyone else". Churchill and Eisenhower had both issued warnings to France not to create a situation which would make the E.D.C. impossible and national armies, including a German national army, the inevitable alternative.

Further difficulties were arising on the French political horizon which were to threaten the European Defence Community, although in the meantime, the E.D.C. had been made a condition according to which the German Treaty establishing a West-German sovereignty, the abolition of the so-called Occupation Statute, would only become operative at the same time as the implementation of the E.D.C.

The German Treaty was signed in May, 1952. By August, 1954 France had not even submitted the E.D.C. Treaty to the French National Assembly. This meant that despite a treaty granting Germany sovereignty having been signed solemnly on the Petersberg by Britain, France, the United States and Germany, the Allied occupation statute was still in force. Neither the German government nor the German parliament were really able to function freely and cope with the many problems Adenauer had outlined in his Berne speech, despite the fact that a parliament had been made possible through the holding of general elections. The German opposition parties were getting restive, especially the Socialists who, curiously enough, assuming the role of nationalists, were beginning to attack Adenauer in aggressively nationalist speeches and repeating such injurious personal attacks as again labelling him "the Chancellor of the Allies".

Britain and the United States did all possible to speed matters. Anthony Eden indicated Britain's readiness to place a British division under E.D.C. command, so that the French would not feel too alone in a joint command with their German partners. John Foster Dulles of the United States threatened to cut off military aid to France unless she moved on E.D.C. French cabinets had succeeded each other, but no progress was made and Adenauer's situation became ever more difficult at home, as everybody's patience, except his own, seemed daily to get more frayed, and the German parliament became increasingly irked with the Occupation

Statute still in force, when in fact all governments had already agreed that it should be substituted by German Sovereignty.

Mendès-France took over as Premier in 1954. His main preoccupation was to extricate France from the disastrous war in Indochina. Adenauer put out feelers whether in view of the continuing delays the German Treaty could not be ratified independently of E.D.C. To Adenauer the E.D.C. was still the best guarantee for a united Europe, without national armies but with joint defences. But the Occupation Statute was most irksome to Germany and most unsatisfactory also to other nations who were anxious to pursue a general reconstruction of Europe's economy and political future.

In August Mendès-France submitted no less than sixty amendments to the Brussels meeting of the E.D.C. states, who were anxious to meet any additional French requirements, if at all possible. For some ten days the ministers struggled to find a solution, particularly the chairman host Paul Henri Spaak of Belgium. No solution was found, since almost every French demand basically opposed a European community and was aimed at lessening French obligations in favour of more and more national integration.

On August 20th the French National Assembly voted on the E.D.C., killing it with a negative vote of 319 to 264. It was an indirect vote on procedure, because the Assembly accepted the "question préalable", which meant that the E.D.C. was thus removed from the agenda of questions to be debated, a debate which had been planned for August 27th, and thus meant its rejection.

One of De Gasperi's greatest political disappointments was the French rejection of the E.D.C. De Gasperi had laboured for it as one of the key guarantees for European peace and he considered that if a Central European Defence were possible, it would mean the disappearance of national armies and lessen the possibility of the rise of nationalism in its old and dangerous form. He had full support from Konrad Adenauer and also from other European members of the community. Britain was backing it through the efforts of Anthony Eden, but it all seemed insufficient. To De Gasperi the E.D.C. was the first stepping stone to the establishment of a political authority in a federated Europe, the cause he himself had championed at Strasbourg where it was then accepted by his French colleagues.

De Gasperi had resigned in July, 1953 and by August 1954 he was a very sick man. He had become President of the Coal and Steel Community, but in fact had practically retired to his native North, living at Valsugana, although he was still in very close touch with the Christian Democrat party in Rome.

On August 14th, he wrote a letter to Fanfani, then Secretary of the party. "If the news which came today from France is true, even if only half true, it would seem that the cause of the E.D.C. has been lost and has detracted some of the lustre from the European Union. That such a decisive and universal cause should still become an object of contention between ministers, between groups of democrats and groups of nationalists, who are still dreaming of the military glories of their emperors, is really a desolate and sad indication of the future.

"You can hardly imagine the pain I feel, particularly as I can no longer raise my voice, in order to at least dissociate my country from any co-responsibility for this calamity. . . . And now, mind this well: Adenauer can maybe swallow such rude set-backs for two reasons. Firstly, he must dissimulate such a defeat because if he admits it, it would immediately lead to the dangerous crumbling of his domestic position; secondly, whatever final form the E.D.C. takes, it will be in some form or another a matter of German rearmament, and it is this which really is of great importance, in the question of an eventual German re-unification as well as in Adenauer's dealings with America. After all, the proposals of Mendès-France imply maintenance of defences on the Elbe River, resistance to Russian attacks and the granting to Germany of a certain army."

"But above all it looks, according to the papers, as if the French are trying to establish a provisional situation", De Gasperi continued, "to escape from an embarrassment and to keep their hands free for a change of front tomorrow. They want to save the Atlantic system (NATO) to-day but at the same time reserve the right to abandon it tomorrow. It is all based on the mistrust, the extreme mistrust towards those nations which are today being called upon to work out common defences".[1]

Written by De Gasperi, a few days before he died in 1954, this was almost prophetic. France under de Gaulle, some twelve years later, asked the NATO establishments in France to leave, and the headquarters were moved from Fontainbleau to Brussels.

During his last days De Gasperi was frequently on the telephone with Paolo Canali. He also telephoned other political friends, urging extreme efforts, if at all possible, to defeat Mendès-France's scuttling of the E.D.C., literally putting the last strength he had into his efforts for European unification, his vision for the peace for which he had striven.

[1] *De Gasperi, Uomo Solo,* Maria Romano Catti De Gasperi (Mondadori, Milan).

On August 19th, 1954, this great champion of world peace and European unity was dead. On August 30th the French Assembly killed the E.D.C.

It was naturally a moment of deep humiliation for Adenauer also. Some of his feelings are reflected in the interview which was reported in the *London Times* on September 4th, when he asked the rhetorical question, "What are the Germans saying now?" and answered:

"They are saying something like this: Stresemann negotiated with Briand, Brüning negotiated with Daladier, and Adenauer negotiated with Schuman—all to no purpose. Must we now assume that the French do not wish for this understanding between our two countries?" Adenauer then turned to the new generation and claimed that the former narrow concept of nationalism had been displaced by a European idea, but if the European idea was to be wrecked by France's action, it was more than possible that exaggerated nationalism might return to Germany. "I do not mean a return to the Nazism of Hitler", Adenauer said, "but a return certainly to some form of nationalism. If Germany is rebuffed by the West and wooed by the East, a new nationalism will look to the Soviet Union. . . . The new nationalism will take years to evolve, but do not let us underrate its beginnings. It is quite clear to me that the Russians will be only too happy to encourage a German nationalism which is looking to the East.

"If some French circles think that with the help of Russia they can play a decisive role in Germany, they are making the same mistake as Beneš (of Czechoslovakia). I do not regard France as lost to the West, and I still hope that she will recover her greatness, and that the European Defence Community will yet come into being. . . . The conception of Europe cannot be killed by a procedural manoeuvre in the French National Assembly with the help of a hundred Communists".

Adenauer was then asked what would come next, and said: "There is only one answer: The Federal Republic must now obtain its full sovereignty, the Occupation Statute cannot be sustained nine years after the war. And implicit in sovereignty is the right of self defence. We are not asking for the right of rearmament as such, but only as part of our sovereignty". Like Adenauer's Berne speech, this *Times* interview stirred up a great deal of argument, but it also stirred up enough attention to break the stalemate.

On September 9th, the six E.D.C. signatories met in London together with Great Britain, the U.S.A. and Canada. It was proposed to extend the Brussels Treaty of 1948 to include Germany, and in this way compensate for the E.D.C. which the French

National Assembly had killed. Mendès-France was told by Anthony Eden that unless agreement on a substitute for E.D.C. could be reached, Britain would no longer feel bound by her former guarantees to France. "Is France willing to forego British support?" he pointedly asked Mendès-France. Nevertheless, even to bring this substitute about took long hours and much effort. The role Anthony Eden played in finding a solution was one of skill and patience. The main differences had to be hammered out between Adenauer and Mendès-France. Once, at a British Embassy dinner in Brussels, when problems again arose which threatened to lead to an impasse, Eden asked Adenauer and Mendès-France to go into an adjoining salon. This time France had injected the Saar question as a condition for accepting points the others had already accepted. While Adenauer and Mendès-France went into the library, Eden sat on a chair outside the door. He actually sat there until three in the morning. When the two men emerged, visibly exhausted, an agreement had been reached. With the ratification of the Western European Union by France on September 13th, 1954 by a slim majority of only twenty-seven votes, the Occupation Statute was finally abolished and Adenauer became Chancellor of a sovereign Federal Republic on May 5th, 1955, when all the various ratifications were deposited in Bonn at a ceremony with the Allied High Commissioner calling on Konrad Adenauer at the Schaumburg Palace. In his official proclamation on that occasion, Adenauer recalled that: "Today, almost ten years after the military and political collapse of National Socialism, the era of occupation ends in the Federal Republic. . . . A free nation ourselves, we have taken our place amongst the free nations of the world, bound to former occupation powers in genuine friendship. . . . There is for us only one place in the world—side by side with the free nations. Our goal is: A free and united Germany in a free and united Europe".

But the struggle for that Europe was no longer a matter merely of reintegrating a rehabilitated Germany. Adenauer had succeeded in rehabilitating Germany domestically and internationally. But it only made sense to him if a rehabilitated Germany could be integrated into a united Europe. Here the real struggle had moved across the Rhine, to France, which was in the throes of an ever-deepening domestic crisis.

It was in Messina, Italy, on June 2nd, 1955 that the first conference took place between the six countries of the Steel and Coal Agreement which had foreseen an extension of those agreements towards a wider European union.

De Gasperi was dead. Schuman had left the French Cabinet, although he was still a member of parliament.

The very first paragraph of the resolution summed up both the purpose and the origin of the Common Market, namely the basic objective of the Schuman Plan: "The governments of Germany, Belgium, France, Italy, Luxembourg and the Netherlands believe the time has come to mark another milestone in the construction of Europe. It is believed that this must be achieved first of all in the economic domain".

Pinay, then Pineau and later Edgar Faure were the French Foreign Ministers throughout the negotiations which lasted several years. Heinrich von Brentano for Germany, Martino for Italy, Bech for Luxembourg, with Bayen and Paul Henri Spaak alternating for Belgium were the men who carried forward the work begun by Schuman, Adenauer and De Gasperi, Adenauer still actively promoting the policy as German Chancellor.

As in the case with the Schuman Plan, England again refused to become part.

The Treaty of Rome, which included Euratom, the joint atomic development, was signed on March 25th, 1957. Paul Henri Spaak describes the treaty in terms which Schuman or De Gasperi or Adenauer would have found inadequate. Spaak says in his memoirs: "The final objectives were to create a Europe, not a satellite of the United States, but as a worthy partner of those in the Western World organised and united for a certain way of life".

The three men who had started Europe on the way to union sought not to defend merely a way of life, but to defend a concept of man, whose way of life in itself was to be but an expression of a higher purpose, a means to achieve a transcendental end. The end alone gave dignity and purpose to life, not its standard of living. They fought for a Christian society whereas Paul Henri Spaak, a great statesman who had contributed much in support of these three men, only saw, as an avowed agnostic, the standard of living as an end itself.

But the actual Treaty gave profound satisfaction to Robert Schuman, whose parliamentary career was drawing to a close. When the Treaty was before the French Assembly, he received an urgent plea from Adenauer to rally parliamentary support against the rising onslaught which had been launched by the Gaullists and Communists against further integration of Europe, an onslaught on all fronts against the Fourth Republic which was soon to fall.

When the Rome Accords, better known as the Common Market, were finally ratified by France on July 10th, 1957 with 352 against 293 votes, the 248 articles, four appendixes, eleven protocols and nine annexes ushered in a new European era. It had been the second step envisaged by the Schuman Plan. That it was passed and implemented was largely due to the enthusiasm which these three men had generated for a European federation and which had not yet exhausted itself. There had, however, been moments of doubt even in Schuman's mind.

At a press conference in Ottawa, on the occasion of a NATO meeting, in 1951, I had had a private chat with Schuman and we arranged for a meeting next morning at the Windsor Hotel in Montreal.

Schuman was anxious for some fresh air and suggested we take a stroll while discussing certain questions. We left the high security area of the hotel where the delegates were lodged and lost ourselves in the morning street crowd along St. Catherine Street. Schuman was extremely concerned with the turn events were taking and the formidable opposition he was experiencing from political opponents of his economic and general unification plans to safeguard peace, not only in Europe but for the world.

"If things don't work out there will be nothing left for me to do but to enter a monastery so as better to pray for the world", Schuman said with frankness and gravity.

Several years later, after the Common Market had been established, Schuman had retired from active politics and his health was visibly failing, we met again, this time on the Piazza Santa Maria Novella in Florence. I had just come out from my hotel, La Minerva, and saw him slowly ambling by, very much aged, accompanied by a niece who was watching over him carefully.

"M. le président", I greeted him, "it pleases me to see that you are not in orders but are still wearing a tie". He seemed somewhat surprised at my unexpected remark, till I recalled our conversation on St. Catherine Street. He smiled reassuringly, commenting that there was ground today for hope, since the dangers of 1951 had grown less. Communism had its own internal problems and the European idea was taking root. "But, remember, there is still great need to pray".

That was our last meeting.

In France, European pessimism had already replaced much of the European hope of earlier days. In the debate on European Accords in Paris on January 15th, 1957 Mendès-France expressed what de Gaulle a little later re-emphasised. Mendès-France said: "France should not become the victim of a treaty. A democracy abdicates in abandoning itself to a dictatorship at home, and also by delegating its powers to an agency outside". It was the former French Premier, Paul Reynaud, who was led to compare Mendès-France's "European pessimism" to Dr. Purgon in Molière's *Malade Imaginaire*, whose patient could only progress from bad to worse in the assured expectation that he would eventually become incurable.

When future biographers recount Adenauer's years of successful struggle to build his country and integrate Europe, they will have to note how his following years in office were strongly influenced by the developments in France. They will have to recount how, when the Fourth Republic fell and de Gaulle came to power with his idea no longer of an integrated Europe, but of a "Europe of fatherlands", Adenauer understood how to skilfully establish close personal relations. He signed a special treaty of friendship with de Gaulle, who visited Germany and gave speeches of cordiality which, on the record of his former policies, were attributed rather to Adenauer's influence than de Gaulle's own previous beliefs. As Adenauer first lost an ally in the death of Alcide De Gasperi and later in the end of Robert Schuman's career, he struggled on alone.

He was the only one of the three who was still at the head of a government. He was the only one in the position of power to defend what the three had been laboriously constructing together over the years. In a way the years ahead were years in which he was left to defend Europe against a renascent French nationalism under de Gaulle, and able to count only on passive support from post-De Gasperi Italian governments, preoccupied with their own domestic uncertainties and constantly facing Cabinet crises. These were years in which two champions of opposing forces were engaged in peaceful but unrelenting efforts for the primacy of their respective ideas. Adenauer was fighting for Europe and, beyond Europe, for an international solidarity of federated states, De Gaulle will go down in history as the champion of orthodox and discredited nationalism which was trying to make a comeback in order to prevent any encroachment on the old-fashioned idea of national sovereignty.

Adenauer and de Gaulle belonged to two entirely distinct and even opposed schools of thought, but Adenauer had one advantage over his younger French contemporary. What de Gaulle faced in the France of 1945 onward, Adenauer had already seen and dealt with in his political experience. Adenauer had struggled courageously against the nascent nationalism in Germany under the Weimar Republic of post-1918 and the emergence of National Socialism. Under Hitler Adenauer had seen the futility of nationalism as a means of solving the problems of modern society. Both de Gaulle and Adenauer had to deal with parliamentary democracy which was conceived on majority principles and which did not function under all circumstances. Adenauer saw the breakdown of majority parliamentary democracy in the Germany of the Weimar Republic and de Gaulle could observe it both in the

French Third Republic before World War II and in the French Fourth Republic immediately afterwards.

In a way both men had to deal in their respective countries with what has been called the "crisis of parliamentary legitimacy". What is a legitimate government, what is treason and what is loyalty when majority rule becomes the supreme criterion? A French writer discussing a national collective, or state, wrote that the day on which each political faction in a parliament chooses its own ideology, which then becomes the supreme criterion for its actions, there is no more national unity. And when that day comes, "there are no more traitors. Each different party with outside links to those with similar ideologies reciprocates with the same epithet of traitor to accusations of treason from its political opponents".[1]

When majority rule takes over as supreme, it must always presuppose basic agreements on political principles by political society as a whole. Otherwise there is a clash of ideologies and that often leads to civil war. If there is a consensus on the values and on the value of social order, which is expressed in nationality, then a few individuals opposing this order in favour of another ideology, can easily and by common consent be designated as traitors, and their actions against the collective become treason. But when a number of such traitors of yesterday begin to represent a large percentage, say 15% or 25% of the members of the society called a state, they become a minority and their anti-national policies of yesterday are termed the political plank of an opposition party. But it is not an ordinary opposition willing to present the state with an alternative government to safeguard the basic structure of the state. It must not be forgotten that both in the Weimar Republic and in the French Third and Fourth Republics the struggle was not merely for the political primacy of a party, but for the destruction of a regime which was bitterly opposed by many parties for different reasons and on ideological lines.

At the time of the Weimar Republic, I had opportunities to witness debates in the Berlin Reichstag and, a few days later, debates in the British House of Commons in London. The consensus on basic traditional values to be upheld in the British parliament led to a spirited debate on methods to safeguard them: a British constitutional monarchy, the maximum of personal liberty guaranteed, except for treason and other crimes, and the pursuit of a foreign policy largely based on common consent.

In the Reichstag of the early Thirties, before Hitler's dictatorship, debates on methods were studies in futility. Before one could talk

[1] *An Introduction to A. Therive's Essai sur la Trahison*, Raymond Aron (Calman, Levy).

of methods to safeguard something, there must be agreement on what to safeguard. There was utter disagreement in the Reichstag on what kind of society to safeguard, what values to uphold. The monarchists, the republicans, the advocates of totalitarian dictatorship, those of nineteenth century liberalism and the libertarians of the twentieth century conservatives, those advocating a strong centralised government and those federalists defending state rights through decentralisation, were only some of the diametrically opposed factions while the existing state could only muster a minority vote for its supporters.

It was the break-down of parliamentary democracy, culminating in Hitler's dictatorship, war and defeat, which Adenauer had witnessed. But he saw it all happen before World War II largely as a direct result of World War I frustrations. He saw parliamentary upheavals in Germany which apparently bore in them the seed of their own destruction.

De Gaulle saw very much the same parliamentary situation arise in France after World War II. When years later I witnessed debates in the French National Assembly of the Fourth Republic, frightening parallels with the Weimar Republic were discernible. The France of 1945 had reached a stage politically, economically and socially not unlike the Germany of 1918. I say "not unlike" rather than "similar" advisedly because the differences were obviously many. Both nations sought to remedy frustrations by evading facts in constructing their nationalistic psychological palliatives which inevitably terminated in a fixation on treason. In other countries government critics would merely have been a political opposition.

The Germans concentrated their enmity on the "international Marxist" and later on the "international Jew" in the post-World War I period, while the French in the post-World War II period first blamed the Communists and the treason of Thorez, and later found scapegoats, like Marshal Pétain and Pierre Laval and other "collaborators" whose respective services to France as patriots in earlier years, and sometimes even under German occupation, were overlooked, to justify the myth of an "untarnished grandeur". Economic suffering and the consequent outside aid both countries needed and had to accept, left serious psychological residues of hurt national pride and consequent fear of foreign economic domination.

The loss of German colonies, through military amputations by victorious Western military might, was probably easier to bear for the Germans of 1918 than the loss of their colonies by the French through military defeat by their own colonials, whether in Indochina, Algiers, Morocco or elsewhere. The loss of German colonies brought the Germans up against the stark realities of military facts. The French had the painful awakening that the *Union Française* was but a French dream, proved by the colonials themselves to be but self-delusion.

As Fieldmarshal von Hindenburg became a symbol to the Germans of a glory which was once theirs and might be brought back again, so General de Gaulle assumed similar proportions in the mind of the French, incorporating the memory of former greatness and the illusion of having carried some of this greatness forward as a visible heritage for the future. With the advent of de Gaulle in France (a Hindenburg rather than a Hitler) as saviour of a foundering French ship of state, Adenauer was suddenly confronted with a statesman and a phenomenon he had known a quarter of a century ago in Germany.

But Adenauer was seeking new forms, because the old European nationalism had died, even if de Gaulle had not yet realised that. In France he was confronted with a man who had preserved for himself the rigid concept of a country that had survived dire hardships, a concept that few of the hardships were of France's own making, but attributable mainly to treason and the failures of bad Frenchmen and faithless foreign allies. In 1945 de Gaulle believed he still stood where Raymond Poincaré and Clemenceau had stood in 1918 with a victorious, even if wounded, France which he, de Gaulle, would again rehabilitate to glories which belonged to past ages.

Adenauer watched the tragic course Germany embarked on when it tried "rehabilitation" rather than integration into the greater unit of international cooperation. The League of Nations was soon denounced by the Germans as a means to rob Germany of her sovereignty, almost in the same terms as de Gaulle denounced first the E.D.C. and later NATO and tried to undermine the workings of a European Common Market. Adenauer sought to learn from the past to avoid its mistakes, but de Gaulle lived in a past which he tried to recreate—including all the recriminations against former enemies such as Germany or allies such as Britain or the United States, who had all "done France wrong".

When the Fourth Republic crumbled and de Gaulle seized power, France was on the verge of economic collapse. It was Adenauer who stepped in, and placed the bulging coffers of the German Bank at de Gaulle's disposal to save the franc, while London and Washington hesitated. What was even more, he accepted French political leadership, even under de Gaulle, in order to save the development on the European Common Market, believing like Schuman, that not politics, but economic realities could forge lasting ties. He had announced his retirement, being well past the age for the bitter struggles he had been through and which were still ahead. But he returned to the chancellorship to save Franco-German relations, when his Economics Minister and heir-apparent Erhard pursued a course which would have estranged Paris from Bonn by humouring London. Adenauer hence postponed his retirement and devoted his last years to Franco-German understanding, even against de Gaulle's determination to bolster French sovereignty at the expense of European consolidation.

When Adenauer finally ceded to Erhard, a formula had been found in the Franco-German Treaty of Consultation. It was true that the treaty was more a declaration of intent, but even that was important and proved particularly useful on the succession in the chancellorship of Kurt Kiesinger and even Willy Brandt. The treaty was a sort of safety valve. The sky was still clouded, but the immediate danger of a storm which could have broken the ten years' bond between Paris and Bonn, a bond which alone would hold together the Europe which Adenauer, Schuman and De Gasperi foresaw, had been weathered, with Konrad Adenauer still at the helm.

It is important to note in connection with Adenauer's vision of a united Europe that he liked to look beyond the immediate danger of a defensive alliance against aggressive Russia. He was actually asked once whether his efforts were aimed against Russia. He denied this vehemently, as Schuman had done earlier in connection with the Schuman Plan. Adenauer pointed to the fact that he himself had visited Moscow and would never have done that unless he hoped in some way to extend international cooperation well beyond the limitations of an East–West struggle. It was only against militant atheistic Communism which expressed itself in the disregard for individual freedoms and national independence—something which never excluded interdependence—that he felt the strength of Western Christian civilisation should at all times be on the alert. Once aggressive designs no longer existed, then not only peaceful accords with the Russian people would be desirable, but would be necessary and even obligatory in the greater search for world peace. But aggression was still manifestly present in Moscow's actions towards its satellites when they try to become freer, as illustrated in Poland, Hungary and Czechoslovakia.

Time alone will tell how deeply the seeds sown by these men—Adenauer, De Gasperi and Schuman—have taken roots. But the biographers will not be able to ignore the role these men played when they pitched, not only their wits or political abilities, but their profound Christian conviction and unflinching faith against the ideology and military might, against the danger of Communist Moscow in the Europe of 1945 and in subsequent years. It was on the strength of this conviction, and other men's trust in those who had conviction, that work could commence on the foundation to be laid for a free society, a moral and Christian democracy. Time will show whether that freedom will live, because the faith of these men will live on to safeguard freedom. Freedom can never be contrived, only freely and fervently accepted.

Bibliography

Alcide De Gasperi Nella Politica Estera Italiana, Adstans (Paolo Canali) (Mondadori, Milan).

De Gasperi E Il Suo Tempo, Giulio Andreotti (Mondadori, Milan).

De Gasperi Uomo Solo, Maria Romana Catti De Gasperi (Mondadori, Milan).

Testimonianze per Alcide De Gasperi, Capelli Editore.

Alcide De Gasperi, Elisa Carillo (Palm Publishers, Montreal).

Il Vaticano E La Guerra, Alberto Giovanetti (Libreria Editrice Vaticana).

Roma Città Aperta, Alberto Giovanetti (Editrice Ancora, Milano).

Le Saint Siège et La Diplomatie, Igino Cardinale (Desclée, Tournai).

I Cattolici Dall'Opposizione Al Governo, Alcide De Gasperi (Laterza, Bari).

A Political History of Post War Italy, Norman Kogan (Praeger, New York).

Diario 1939–43, Galeazzo Ciano (Rizzoli, Milan), vols. I and II.

The Social Doctrine of the Catholic Church, Emile Guerry (Palm Publishers, Montreal).

Erinnerungen, Konrad Adenauer (Deutsche Verlagsanstalt, Stuttgart), Vol. I, 1945–1953; Vol. II, 1953–1955; Vol. III, 1955–1959; Vol. IV, 1959–1963.

Adenauer und das Neue Deutschland, Edgar Alexander (Paulus Verlag, Recklinghausen).

Adenauer, Edgar Alexander, (Farrar Straus and Cuddahy, New York).

Adenauer, Paul Weymar (André Deutsch, London).

Der Bundeskanzler (Dirkreiter Verlagsgesellschaft, Freiburg i/Br.).

L'Allemagne d'Adenauer, Robert d'Harcourt (Flamarion, Paris).

The Nazi Persecution of the Churches, J. S. Conway (Weidenfeld & Nicolson, London).

20 Juli, Bundeszentrale für Heimatdienst (Herder, Freiburg i/Br).

Bismarck, A. J. P. Taylor (Random House, New York).

Contemporary Europe: A History, H. Stuart Hughes (Prentice-Hall, New York).
Soldatentum und Rebellion, Gert Buchheit (Grote, Rastatt).
On Borrowed Time, Leonard Moseley (Random House, New York).
Robert Schuman, Robert Rochefort (Cerf, Paris).
Pour L'Europe, Robert Schuman (Nagel, Paris).
La IVième République et sa Politique Extérieur, Alfred Grasser (Armand Colin, Paris).
La République des Contradictions, 1951–1954, Georgette Elgey (Fayard, Paris).
La IVième République, Jacques Fauvet (Fayard, Paris).
Pendant la Guerre, 1940–1946, Charles de Gaulle (Plon, Paris).
Dans l'Attente, 1946–1958, Charles de Gaulle (Plon, Paris).
Avec le Renouveau, 1958–1962, Charles de Gaulle (Plon, Paris).
Pour l'Effort, 1962–1965, Charles de Gaulle (Plon, Paris).
Vers le Terme, 1966–1969, Charles de Gaulle (Plon, Paris).
La Grande Conférence, Jacques Bourbon-Bousset (Gallimard, Paris).
The Schuman Plan, William Diebold jr. (Praeger, New York).
Combats Inachevés, Paul-Henri Spaak (Fayard, Paris) Vols. I and II.
With Malice Toward None, Cecil King (Sidgwick & Jackson, London).
Memoirs of the Second World War, Winston Churchill, Kelly (Houghton Mifflin, Boston).
Modern Europe, Roger L. Williams (St. Martin's, New York).
The History of Germany Since 1789, Golo Mann (Chatto & Windus, London).
The Meaning of Treason, Rebecca West (The Viking Press, New York).
Germany's Underground, Allen W. Dulles (Macmillan, New York).
Western Europe Since 1945, D. W. Urwin (Longmans, London).

INDEX

1 **Figures in bold type indicate that the subject is discussed in some detail, or is of particular significance.**

2 Relationships to Konrad Adenauer (KA), Alcide De Gasperi (DG) and Robert Schuman (RS) are shown in square brackets following the name.